THE VITAL CONNECTION

Written by

John Goldingay

Edited and designed by

David Muir

Cartoons by

Taffy

Published by **St John's Extension Studies**
Bramcote, Nottingham NG9 3RL

ISBN 1-900920-06-9

Printed in Great Britain by AT Print, Rotherham.

CONTENTS

WHO THIS BOOK IS FOR

This workbook is for people who want their spiritual life, their life in relation to God, to be better. People may define that 'better' in very different ways – more fulfilling, more honest, more faithful, more intimate, more empowering for ministry, more relevant, more biblical, more like Jesus. Whatever that particular 'more' is, they have one thing in common – a desire to move on with God.

Some may be wanting to move on in what they feel is a relatively good spiritual life – good but perhaps rather stuck on a plateau. They know that being a Christian is being a pilgrim, and are looking for a resource that will help them keep on the move.

Others may be anticipating a more demanding life ahead of them as Christians – perhaps preparing for a new phase in Christian service, or entering a life change such as marriage. Will the resources of the past be adequate to meet the new challenges? Or will the demands ahead reveal weaknesses that will come back to haunt us?

Others again may have a sense of helplessness, even hopelessness, about the future direction of their life with God. They may feel they have rather lost their way spiritually, or particular moral or spiritual failures may have left them lacking clear direction in their Christian lives.

This workbook is for all of these, and many others. What they have in common is a desire to see change and development in their relationship with God. In fact, they are all on the same journey – and outward appearances on how 'far on' we are on that journey are notorious deceptive.

Knowledge about the spiritual life is important, and you will certainly acquire some of that as you work through the book. But this workbook is not *about* spirituality; its primary aim is not to make you more knowledgeable. It is *for* spiritual growth; it offers you a process for consolidating and developing your life with God. It is like a marriage enrichment process – the focus is on the heart more than on the head. If you merely wish to become more knowledgeable about spirituality, you will find this workbook frustrating. But if you want knowledge that you can use to develop your life with God, you will find this workbook accessible and useful to that end.

HOW TO USE THIS BOOK

We have written into this workbook a process of spiritual review, beginning in Unit 1 and culminating in Unit 8. We commend this process to those who are looking for an overall review of their life with God. Such a review is likely to require some help from someone with a mature Christian faith, even someone experienced in 'spiritual direction', and we recommend that you identify such a person and work through the workbook process with them. If you need help in identifying someone, your minister should be able to refer you. They may offer to take on this role themselves.

As well as someone to talk to, you might benefit from someone more distant, someone who could help you review your spiritual life 'from afar'. This perspective can also be very useful. For this reason we offer to provide support for this module from St John's Nottingham. Such a 'tutor' would invite you to undertake particular pieces of reflective writing on your spiritual development, and would suggest other resources you might refer to. They would also help you identify a suitable local person to talk to. There is a form at the end of the workbook to enable you to request this support.

Having said all that, we have also designed the workbook so that it is easy to dip into at almost any point. You can 'graze' through the workbook looking for things that may help you. You can identify from the contents page a Unit which seems to meet a particular need at present. The spiritual life is partly at least about 'inspiration' – and a little insight bedded into one of the pages of this workbook might act for you as an inspiration for significant spiritual growth. If it does, we will feel that the time and energy put into making the book as accessible as this has been worthwhile. Remember, it is a workbook - so don't be afraid to write in it!

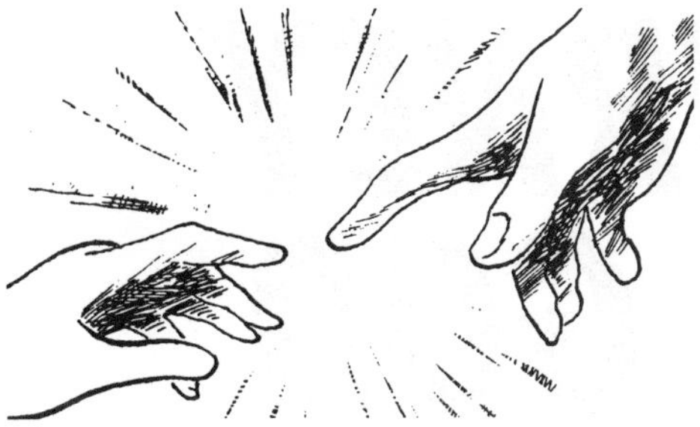

Unit 1

REVIEW YOUR ROOTS

PURPOSE

This Unit introduces the idea of 'spirituality', and asks what it really is.

It also invites you to become aware of the roots of your own Christian faith, why you are the kind of Christian you are. It invites you to move on from there, because faith is always a journey. It also helps you come to terms with what you might (perhaps sadly) be leaving behind.

CONTENTS

A JOURNEY WITH GOD

I can still recall my 50th birthday. Some people looked at me knowingly ('It's a big one, 50'). The look implied I must be going through a crisis. All I remember was thinking that I was now twice as old as when I was 25...

Whatever age you are, you are on a journey. This workbook is designed to be a stimulus on that journey – to help it be a journey that has direction. It is also designed to help you look at the journey you have already been travelling, and to see where you have been.

25 + 25

By the time I was 25, I had grown up, left home, been ordained, fallen in love, and (nearly) got married. Subconsciously I reckoned that all the significant things in my life had now happened. I half-knew that becoming a parent in due course would be a pretty shattering experience, but I assumed that by the age of 25 I was formed as a person and as a Christian. All there would be for the next 25 years was more of the same.

Looking back from my 50th birthday, I almost laughed. Nothing could have been further from the truth. Outwardly very little happened to me over the next 25 years. I stayed married to the same person, and for 22 years stayed working in the same place – both of which were unadventurous by contemporary standards. But in the ongoing story of who I am, of what I make of life, of how I relate to people, and of how I relate to God, I have continuously been on a journey.

I also realized that there was no reason why that 'journeying' should not continue for as long as I lived. I had looked at people in their 60s and 70s whose bodies were getting a bit frail and stiff, and I had assumed that their spirits too were probably getting stale and tired. I realized that this is often not so at all. That made me excited about the future – it was not all downhill from here.

THE NOVELIST AND THE THEOLOGIAN

I recently read an interview with a novelist I much enjoy. He had passed his 60th birthday, and he commented that he now had to do more research for his novels because he didn't have so much new experience to resource his writing.

I thought, 'What a shame!' What a contrast with the great contemporary theologian Jürgen Moltmann who was almost 70 when he visited St John's. But new things were still happening to him, and he was still thinking new theological thoughts.

Shaped by life

The day before I started writing this workbook, my wife Ann had a downwards lurch in the effects of her multiple sclerosis. Two days later, she was admitted to a rehabilitation centre. Eventually she returned home but the crisis is repeated frequently. Ann and I have been living with that kind of experience since just before I was 25, and that has decisively shaped my journey as a human being and as a Christian.

You may not have something like that shaping you (please God). But you will have other things that *are* shaping you. What happens to you in your relationships, in your work and in other experiences and aspects of life, influences who you are and how you relate to God. These experiences raise questions for you – and bring out potentials in you.

Broadened by experience

I wish I had kept a journal about the significant things that happened to me. The nearest I have to such a journal is my sermon notes. I looked back at some recently, and I could see both the continuity and the change.

In one sense the changes I would need to make in order to re-preach some Bible exposition I delivered in the 1970s would be trivial. But in another sense what I had understood about the Bible, about the Christian faith, about God, and about me, is now set in a much bigger context. So what I found myself wanting to say to my old notes was 'Yes, but...'

I know I am not alone in having that kind of experience.

- The evangelical writer John Stott changed his mind radically in his 50s about Christian attitudes to the world and to politics. Of course there are continuities. Journeys are like that. John Stott still believed in the same gospel as he did in his 30s. But it was now set in a broader context.
- I know a woman who was brought up a 'Catholic' kind of Christian, and who as she grew up took on more 'Liberal' views. Then she somehow ended up in an Evangelical college. There, not least because of her friendships with people of other convictions and experience, she has come to react to some things in a more 'Evangelical' or 'Charismatic' kind of way. She has not rejected her Catholic or Liberal outlook, but it is now set in a wider context.

I grew up an Evangelical. This gave me a deep appreciation of the Bible, and made the cross of Christ central in my thinking. Then I tip-toed into charismatic renewal, and found new freshness in my relationship to Christ and new ways of prayer and ministry. In addition, I came to appreciate 'Liberal' insights on some aspects of the Christian faith – so I no longer minded if I didn't know the answers to some questions! And I discovered 'Catholic' ways of worshipping and praying, and through that read some of the great 'spiritual writers' such as St John of the Cross.

At the end of all that, by the age of 50 I was more enthusiastic about the Bible than I was when I was 25 – not least because of the way it had shaped me along the journey. As the years go on, in one sense I am the same as I was before. But what I used to be is set in a broader context.

A question of direction

Whether or not you want to be, you *are* on a journey with God. If you do nothing to direct that journey, the journey does not stop – it may go round in circles or plod along unadventurously.

When you start thinking about your relationship with God, as you will do as you study this workbook, you open up the possibility that your journey with God may take new directions. If you think about it, and take your share of responsibility for your life with God, you may have the chance to go somewhere interesting and worthwhile and see new places.

TRACING YOUR JOURNEY

On a sheet of paper list on the left hand side the key events of your life. Let them spread down the whole sheet. Then on the right hand side make some notes on how your relationship with God and your understanding of God developed over the same time. What links can you see?

With hindsight, can you now see further implications for your understanding of God and your relationship with God? Discuss your sheet with a friend if you can.

WHAT IS 'SPIRITUALITY'?

When people want to talk about how their lives relate to God, they sometimes use the term 'spirituality'. 'Spirituality' is a dangerous word because it means different things to different people. And it can sound as if it means things that it doesn't really mean.

My daily newspaper recently included this paragraph:

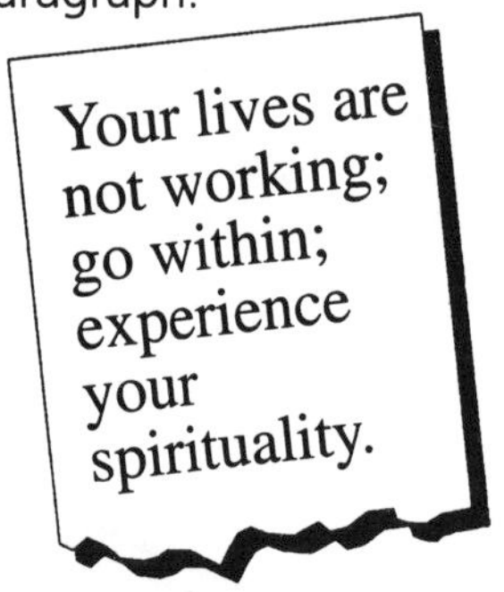
Your lives are not working; go within; experience your spirituality.

The words might have come from a book on *Christian* spirituality, but they are actually the battle cries of the New Age movement, according to this article.

'Spirituality' can sound as if being spiritual really means looking inside you, going into your own depths. It can imply that what you find is the transcendent side to yourself.

Today we are interested in finding our own real selves, finding out who we are, discovering our gifts, developing our potential. We are interested in self-expression, self-fulfilment, being true to ourselves. Your interest in spirituality is in part an aspect of that. You may think it is a Christian matter. You may not realize how far it is a distinctively modern and cultural matter.

New Age people talk of spirituality, as Christians also do. The interest in spirituality in the church corresponds to the interest in the pagan world. So as Christians we need to make sure that our spirituality is *Christian* spirituality and that our thinking about spirituality reflects the nature of the gospel and the patterns of Scripture.

All of life – in the Spirit

Another danger of the word 'spirituality' is that it can sound as if it's only about 'spiritual things' such as prayer. In this workbook we are interested in the *whole* of our life with God. 'Spirituality' *is* about our religious life, the way we *pray* – but it's also about the rest of our life, the way we *live*.

When a person takes religious vows and becomes a monk or a nun, those vows usually involve a commitment to poverty, chastity and obedience. Those three vows link with the three telling things in life – money, sex and power. Spirituality is about how you live with God in relation to money, sex and power, as well as about how you pray.

That's true for people who take religious vows, but it is also true for the rest of us. Spirituality is about our *inner* lives, the way we think, what happens at the depths of us; but it's also about our *outer* lives, the way we behave in the world. It's about

'Spirituality is nothing less than the whole of life orientated towards God, shaped by God, graced by God.'

Jim Cotter, *Pleasure, Pain and Passion*

how we live those inner and outer lives *with God*.

'Life in the Spirit' would be a better phrase than spirituality. Admittedly it may sound as if it's just to do with charismatic approaches to Christian living. Or, like 'spirituality', it can sound as if it's just to do with the inner person, or just to do with 'spiritual' or religious things.

But 'Life in the Spirit' is a good phrase because it's (almost) a biblical phrase. Spirituality is about 'living according to the Spirit' (the phrase in Romans 8), or 'living by the Spirit' (the phrase in Galatians 5).

And in the Bible the Spirit isn't just concerned about what we call 'spiritual' things. The Spirit is concerned about the inner person *and* the outer person, about the body and the soul. So life in the Spirit is about thinking and prayer – and about behaviour and mission. The Holy Spirit is involved in all those, in the realm of the inner person and in the realm of life in the world.

A journey of questions

I have been a Christian for decades. I have been praying for decades. The way I pray now is different from the way I prayed forty years ago. The person I am is different. The way I think about life in lots of aspects is different. The way I think about God is different.

We all change – not necessarily because we were wrong before or because we want to reject what we were before, but because God wants to do different things with us at different times, and because God doesn't want us to stand still.

This is not an easy journey to take. There are very understandable reasons why we often resist it:

- Scripture tells us to be **faithful** to the traditions handed down. We talk today of narrow-mindedness being a weakness and broad-mindedness being a kind of maturity; but Scripture talks of a 'broad way' that leads to destruction and a 'narrow way' that leads to life. How far can we allow ourselves to be enriched by other traditions, without being unfaithful to our roots?
- We have strong **emotional** attachments to the Christianity we were brought up in or converted into. There is an underlying link between spirituality and our emotions (even the conviction that we should not be emotional in our spiritual life!). What is happening in our hearts when we question our roots? We may be afraid that we will lose something precious.
- It is always **sad** to leave the simplicities of childhood behind, and this is also true of our spiritual childhood. But as we 'grow up' into Christ, we inevitably outgrow some of our spiritual past, and we must live through the sadness of that. If we always back off from the process of 'spiritual adolescence', with its questioning and even rebellion, we may live the whole of our lives without ever discovering spiritual maturity.

The journey starts here

Fortunately God meets us where we are. So if we are preoccupied with the modern passion for spirituality, God will graciously meet us there. And if we are tied strongly to a particular religious past, God will meet us there too.

So expect that God will meet you where you are. But also be prepared that God may want to take you somewhere else.

A BOOK OF ANSWERS?

Thirty years ago there was little talk about spirituality. That doesn't mean people prayed less, but 'spirituality' became an issue in the church in the 1970s. There was a question to which people wanted an answer.

I once went to a conference on the teaching of spirituality. It had a large bookstall with hundreds of books about spirituality. While there were a few classics, most of the books had been published in the last ten years or so. That shows that spirituality is a question which publishers think people are interested in! But it also showed that it's a question to which there isn't a very clear answer...

These books contain partial answers, or answers that help different people at different points in their lives. This workbook is another. As with the other books, you will not find 'the answer' here. Rather, you will find ideas and resources to help you on *your* journey with God.

STRANDS OF SPIRITUALITY

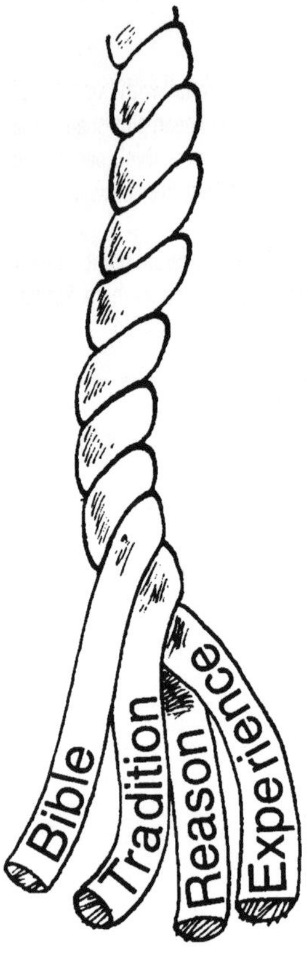

1 is an out-and-out evangelical, averse to the other strands
2 is a catholic with marked charismatic sympathies
3 is a liberal with some catholic sympathies
4 is a charismatic exploring the values of the other strands

Different people have related to God in different ways. Within the Bible, the classic examples are the differences between Abraham and Moses and between Paul and James.

- **Abraham** was called to live by trust in God's promises, and **Paul** loved to emphasize the fundamental importance of *faith* in our relationship with God.
- **Moses** gave Israel vast amounts of instructions about how God expected people to live, and **James** likewise had no time for faith without works.

Abraham and Paul also believed in obedience, of course, and Moses and James believed in faith – but their emphases were different. The same difference is visible in figures such as Luther and Calvin.

There are all sorts of reasons for such differences. They reflect the fact that the truth of God is rich and many-coloured. They reflect personality. They also reflect historical and political questions.

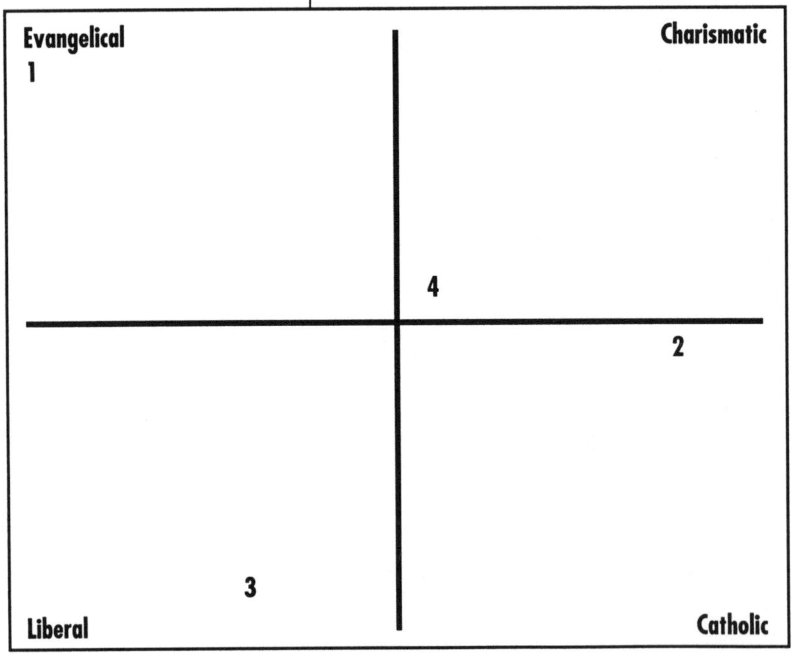

Some of these differences have crystallized into strands of spirituality. We will discuss four. These are not the only spiritual traditions. Later we will look at liberation, feminist, and celtic spiritualities, and for some people these are more important in defining the way they relate to God. The orthodox and the pentecostal could also be added.

The Church has always held together the three strands of Bible, church tradition and reason. More recently we have added religious experience. These four traditions of spirituality relate to four common influences on Christian belief:

- The **evangelical** consciously stresses the Bible
- The **catholic** is more aware of the church's tradition
- The **charismatic** emphasizes the reality of experience of God
- The **liberal** urges the importance of our God-given human reason

You may not identify solely with one of these four traditions, just as we all combine some reliance on the Bible, tradition, reason, and religious experience. They are not mutually exclusive (and the four words are often used in a way which caricatures their meaning) but I think it is helpful (and historically true) to distinguish between them.

As you read on, try to place yourself on the grid. The numbered points on it provide you with examples. See how many features of the different strands apply to you. See how other features intrigue you and make you interested in investigating them.

As well as indicating where you are now, show where you were soon after you became a Christian and at some time in between. What 'route' have you taken across the grid?

1. CATHOLIC

The mystery of God

I am very aware of the awesomeness and holiness of God. I know God cares about me, but God is also transcendent and mysterious. We can't tie God down. When I walk through a majestic cathedral or watch people processing and there is incense swirling about, I appreciate the mystery of the faith. It puts me in touch with the realities of heavenly worship.

You pray. I'll do the incense.

Continuity

Over the centuries God has guided the church with clear authority about what to believe, how to worship, and how to live our lives. I believe in standing firmly in the tradition – the beliefs and ways of worship which have been passed down to us and which link us with Christians through the ages. That doesn't mean that nothing can change; but I expect change to be reclaiming parts of the tradition rather than pure innovation. It is also something that Christians will do *together* rather than unilaterally. I appreciate the fact that the line of bishops and priests puts me in touch with the leaders of the early church and with Jesus himself.

Confessing my sins

I find it helpful to confess my sins to a priest on a regular basis. It makes me take my sins seriously and it challenges me to do something about them. It reassures me when God's appointed servant declares to me that my sins are forgiven and that I am right with God.

Spiritual direction

Every six months I go to see a nun to discuss my spiritual life with her. I tell her how my prayer life and other aspects of my life have been working out. Often, simply articulating all that sets the agenda for the future for me. But sometimes she will ask some devastating question which makes me see something new, or will point out something in my story which enables me to see things more clearly. She may also suggest I read something from a spiritual writer – which sometimes I find helpful, sometimes not!

The church and the eucharist

Being Christian is something that associates me with other people. When I gather with others for the celebration of the Eucharist, Christ is present in a special way. When I receive the bread and wine, I receive Christ in a definite and concrete way. I am assured that God is not remote but very near, part of my very being, because Christ has committed himself to being present in the bread and the wine. So I appreciate it when a church retains some of the bread from the Eucharist and keeps it in church, to symbolize the presence of Christ himself there for me.

The fellowship of heaven

I am aware of belonging to the worldwide and historic communion of saints, and I believe that the saints down the ages have not lost interest in what goes on in the church on earth. So I find it natural to ask them for their prayers. I especially appreciate being able to express gratitude to Mary as our Lord's own mother for what she made possible for us, and to ask her to pray for me.

2. CHARISMATIC

You pray.
I'll catch.

Speaking in tongues

I find myself speaking out or murmuring in 'nonsense' words. Sometimes this is a way of praising God when ordinary words seem inadequate. Sometimes it is a way of praying about something when I don't know how to pray about it.

Experience of God

What attracted me to charismatic spirituality was the strong sense of the reality of God and the possibility of knowing God personally now. Christian faith was not just theological theory, but living experience. In private prayer and in public worship I can express my emotions to God and feel such joy in praise and prayer.

Baptism in the Spirit

I know that I found forgiveness in Christ when I was converted, and found great joy in that. It was as if I started a new life. But over time my sense of the reality of that rather disappeared, and my life with Christ became more routine. Then I had an experience of being overwhelmed by the presence of the Holy Spirit, and it was like starting all over again as a Christian.

Hearing God

I expect God to speak to me. Sometimes this happens to me *directly*, when I am on my own or with other people. I realize that a sentence or an image has come into my mind, which I don't feel I made up. This brings a message to me or to someone else. Sometimes it happens *indirectly*, when someone else tells me of a sentence or picture which they believe God may have given them for me. These kinds of experiences reinforce my conviction that God really is involved in my life.

Healing

I expect God to act as well as to speak. I ask God to bring healing to people who are ill, and I'm glad that people pray for me when I am ill. I believe that sometimes God heals people of serious physical illnesses, though I recognize that often healing is a matter of smaller things. I know that God works on people's spirits through those smaller experiences of healing.

Church and ministry

The experience of God speaking and acting through spiritual gifts such as prophecy, tongues and healing makes for a different attitude to the church and its ministry. I am impatient with the church when it is just a matter of the outward form. All the liturgy may take place according to the right rules but there is no power to it. And I don't believe that ministry is the prerogative of one or two people. It is the task of the whole body of the church. The gifts are distributed throughout that body, and the task of leadership is to free it – not stifle it!

Facing supernatural evil

I believe that evil is more than merely what we see. There are spiritual forces of evil active in the world. We have to recognize these and claim the power of Christ to gain victory over them.

INSTINCTIVE STORIES

- Catholics relate instinctively to the incarnation (so they genuflect or kneel right down at that point in the Creed)
- Liberals relate most to Jesus' teaching ministry (e.g. the sermon on the Mount)
- Evangelicals relate most to the death of Christ (the gospel is the fact that Christ died for us)
- Charismatics relate instinctively to Jesus' healing ministry and to Pentecost

3. EVANGELICAL

The Bible

The Bible is the key resource for my belief and for my spiritual life. Each day I reckon to read a section of it, probably with the aid of some notes (such as those published by Scripture Union). Or I may work through it systematically with the aid of a system (such as *Search the Scriptures*). I expect to discover something about God, something about me, and something that I can put into practice that day. I am suspicious when Christians act on the basis of what they think God has said to them, if it does not comes from Scripture. We should not act on the basis of our own reason, or just because the church says we should.

Grace and faith

The foundation of my life with God is God's grace and love, not anything I do. I don't get into a relationship with God by doing good things, whether it's religious acts such as taking Communion or practical acts such as social action. I am in a relationship with God because God reached out to me. All I had to do was respond with trust in God. I am justified by faith, not by works.

The death of Christ

The gospel centres on the fact that Christ died for me. This is the focus of evangelical hymns – such as 'Just as I am, without one plea, but that thy blood was shed for me' and 'When I survey the wondrous cross'. The basic human problem is that we are sinners and have cut ourselves off from God. The death of Jesus makes it possible for us to be cleansed from sin and to enter God's presence with confidence.

Witness and mission

The fact that Christ died for us is the vital good news for the whole world. There is only one gospel: all religions do not lead to God. So sharing this good news with my family and my friends is one of my first obligations. I am also committed to seeing that this gospel is shared with the whole world, by supporting missionary work abroad.

You pray. I'll look up the reference.

The world to come

People sometimes talk as if Evangelicals are so heavenly-minded as to be no earthly use. I know that this has been true from time to time, but it is not built-in to being Evangelical. I am proud to stand in the tradition of 19th century social activists such as Hannah More and Lord Shaftesbury. At the same time I don't kid myself that we are going to bring in the kingdom of God by our well-meaning activities. Only God can do that, and I am looking forward to Jesus' coming again as the time when God will put down evil and when justice will reign.

Prayer

Each day I spend half an hour having a 'quiet time' with God. Part of the time goes to reading the Bible, the rest to prayer. I often use the ACTS scheme: **A**doration (worshipping God), **C**onfession (examining myself and acknowledging my sins), **T**hanksgiving (giving thanks for God's goodness to me), and **S**upplication (asking for what I need and praying for other people).

INSTINCTIVE SOURCES

- For evangelicals the Bible is their key spiritual resource (so they read it every day)
- For charismatics their own experience of God speaking and acting is of key importance
- For catholics Holy Communion is of special importance (so catholic churches may celebrate Holy Communion every day)
- For liberals the use of their own mind is vital to authentic spirituality (what makes sense is what counts)

4. LIBERAL

You pray.
I'll reflect on what happens.

Freedom to think

Of the Church's four strands, I emphasize the God-given gift of human reason. I believe God wants us to learn from all sources of insight, and I don't think God wants us to believe nonsense. I can't identify with people who rejoice in believing six impossible things before breakfast, or who would happily accept that Jonah swallowed the whale if the Bible told them so. I believe in a thinking faith.

Leaving questions open

When I was a teenager, it was important to me to have the answer to every question about the Christian faith and about morality. Nowadays I don't mind keeping questions open. On a quiet day once, a speaker referred to being rooted and grounded in love, and commented that 'a rooted person can be a questioning person.' As I've got older my roots in God have gone deeper. I can cope with radical questioning about whether the doctrine of the Trinity or of the two natures of Christ means anything, or what we mean about God 'existing' at all.

Being realistic

I want a oneness between what I believe when I am in church saying my prayers, and what I believe when I am living the rest of my life. Much Christian spirituality lives in a ghetto and pretends that things are otherwise than they are. We talk about Jesus having inaugurated the kingdom of God and about us being a new creation, when this is clearly not the case. I believe in being honest with God and with myself.

Open to new insights

I believe God speaks to us through the world, through all the realms of human thought and discovery. We know some things that previous generations didn't know, and it is foolish to live our Christian faith as if we only knew what people in the Bible knew. So if we now know things about human sexuality and come to see things about sexual relationships that other generations did not see, we ought to integrate them into our faith. If people 2000 years ago believed in 'demons', perhaps that was just their way of thinking; it doesn't mean that I have to take that 'picture talk' literally.

Open to other spiritualities

I believe that people other than Christians relate to God, and that we therefore ought to expect to learn from Buddhist spirituality, Jewish spirituality, New Age spirituality, and so on. It also means that I don't feel the need to 'convert' them to my faith, if they know God already.

How God acts

I don't see any evidence that God keeps intervening in our world. Even if God did so in Jesus' ministry or in raising him from the dead, I don't see evidence that this happens now. God has given us the world, and expects us to get on with running it. We are God's grown-up children: God is very interested in what we do, but expects us to live our own lives without God interfering in them. That means I find worshipping God natural enough, but asking God to *do* things in our world is harder.

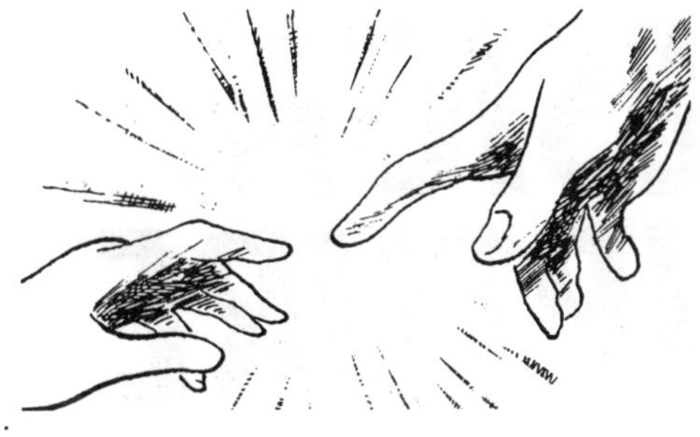

Unit 2

BIBLE SPIRITUALITY

PURPOSE

This Unit is about the Bible and what kinds of 'spirituality' we see in it.

Whatever our Christian background, Scripture is an authoritative source for how God deals with His people. It is a good place to start in reviewing our spiritual lives – but be ready for some surprises…

CONTENTS

THE DESIGN OF SCRIPTURE

Many people have begun reading through the Bible on the assumption that it was designed to feed their relationship with God – and given up in Leviticus because it did not seem to do so. Why didn't it?

Perhaps one reason is that the Bible has other concerns than simply feeding our individual relationship with God (presumably because God has other concerns than that too.)

If the Bible had been designed primarily to be a resource for our spiritual lives, it would have needed to be a different kind of book.

Look at books which *were* written to resource our inner spiritual lives, to see how true that is. Perhaps what God reckons we need to read if our spiritual lives are to develop, is broader than we had thought...

The Bible is not written like a spiritual resource book but it *is* supposed to relate to our life with God. So how does it do that?

The Bible Story

It is no coincidence that the Bible is essentially a story – and basically a factual one rather than a fictional one. It tells us the story of how God created the world, how God related to the people of Israel, and how that led in due course to the emergence from Israel of the key figure in the world's story, Jesus Christ.

That relates to our lives with God in a number of ways.

- Sometimes the story gives us examples of the way people live with God, for us to follow (or the way they fail to live with God, for us to avoid).
- Sometimes it gives us examples of the way God relates to people, which can fire our imaginations regarding the way God may relate to us.
- More importantly, it tells us the large-scale story of how God set about achieving a purpose in the world. It tells us what God was seeking to achieve, and what God did at the story's high-point to make sure it succeeded. If are to relate to God, we need to know something of who God is; and this story tells us the kind of God we have.

Three long Psalms illustrate the way in which Israel related its story to its life with God.

- Psalm 105 suggests that recalling the biblical story is the secret to worship and to obedience.
- Psalm 106 suggests that recalling the story is the secret to being sure that we are forgiven, because the story is one of sin – and then of forgiveness.
- Psalm 107 suggests that recalling the story is the secret to hope.

When you are in the wilderness, in the dark, in sin or in deep water, the biblical story provides you with a counter-story, one you can treat as the ultimate story, one which sets your own, more limited, story in perspective.

Bible Instructions

Somewhat shorter sections of the Bible are occupied with telling people how to live their lives – how to live in relationship to each other, how to organize the economy, how to structure society, how to run the family, how to keep the church in order. This reminds us that spirituality is not just a matter of things going on in our heads and hearts. It is about how we live with God in the world and in the church.

In the Gospels, Jesus' responses to Satan's temptations show how well he knew the instructional parts of Scripture and how to use them. In fact, it turns out that Leviticus is very much about spirituality in the sense of our life with God. Alongside regulations about worship, Leviticus is about houses, family life, war, food, relationships and debt.

Psalm 119 concentrates on the relationship between spirituality and God's precepts and commands. Faithfulness to God is not just a matter of mechanical obedience to rules, but of loving God's word of command (Psalm 119:47-48, 102-4). God's instructions can be loved, in the conviction that they reflect how God's world is and how God is. God's commands have God's reasons behind them.

Bible Promises

Psalm 119 also reflects another aspect of Scripture. As well as telling us how we should behave, the Bible tells us how *God* promises to behave: see Psalm 119:41-42, 49-50, 147-148. In the same way, God's word to Jesus at his baptism invites him to live in the light of God's promises – from a Psalm and from Isaiah (Luke 3:22).

In Psalm 119 the psalmist is praying under pressure (as most of the psalmists do). There is the *external* pressure of being under attack despite being committed to God's ways (or *because* of being committed to God's ways). There is also the *internal* pressure of wondering whether God's word is really true. God's word of promise invites us to be expectant that God will do new things.

Bible Testimonies

A substantial section of the Old Testament, and smaller sections of the New, comprise people's testimony to the way they have prayed and praised, agonized and thanked. This material obviously relates most directly to spirituality in the narrow sense, and we will look at this material in the rest of this Unit.

MIND AND IMAGINATION

Reading Scripture for any purpose involves mind and imagination.

You may question how far you want to use your **mind** in studying Scripture. There can be a tension between asking critical questions and being open to God. But all truth is God's truth, so we needn't be afraid of asking questions, or of living with questions to which we don't yet see the answers.

You may need more **imagination** as you read Scripture. When we are reading Gospel stories, we can be drawn into them imaginatively and live through them as someone actually involved. We can then ask what Jesus is saying to *us* as he speaks to people in the story, or what we would say to him if we were there. When we are reading Psalms with their strong images of water overwhelming us or of God as stronghold, we can enter into the reality of what these images signify.

Let the reading of Scripture involve your whole person.

THE BIBLE AND THE WORLD

Of course God's commands often go against the way the world sees things. What the world says about justice or green issues may seem to fit with Scripture – although Scripture will add to the world's perspective. What it says about money, work, sexuality, drink, family relationships, or possessions may not fit at all. And we need to be aware as Christians that we have often marginalized Scripture's angle on some of these matters because the world's perspective has its attractions...

PRAYING WITH THE PSALMS

We have noted already that 'spirituality' is not confined to prayer. But anybody studying a workbook on 'living with God' probably hopes to learn something about how to pray. Here I am mostly thinking about praying for ourselves (supplication) rather than praying for other people (intercession). There is a whole Unit on intercession later in the workbook.

The Bible's great manual about prayer is the Psalms. Until the present century, the Psalms were *the* place in Scripture from which people learned to pray. In the traditional worship of the Church of England and the Church of Scotland, they were *the* words people used in worship – at that time there were very few hymns. Yet I wonder how far people's own prayers were shaped by the prayers of the Psalms even then?

Shaped by the Psalms?

In the last church service or midweek fellowship group you went to, how did people pray for their own needs? How did you last pray for yourself when you were on your own?

- What did you tell God?
- What did you say about God, and about yourself?
- Were there any ways in which you tried to persuade God to answer – any reasons you reminded God of, why your prayer *should* be answered?
- What did you ask God to *do*?

Write down some answers to these questions. They will help you crystallize how your own or your church's prayer works.

✎ • told God what I felt
what I wanted to feel – peace about the issue
• reminded myself what God is like
– loving, worthy of trust
• I was debating my feelings with God
I wanted his peace – to wait, to trust, to believe I would hear when the moment came
He told me why I was waiting – the struggle was mine

Church – long list of requests linked to scripture / challenge re God

Now read Psalms 42-44. They are really two not three Psalms – Psalms 42 & 43 have the same chorus and seem to be one psalm which has got divided. So you have an example of an *individual* praying (Psalm 42-43) and an example of a *community* praying (Psalm 44). Try asking of these psalms the same questions you asked of your own and your church's prayers.

- How are they similar?
- How are they different?

✎ 42\43 end – in remembrance of good times as an indiv. God addressed
expr trust – [illegible] questioning openness
hope expressed
44 communal memory
expr trust
questioning
call for God to act
both – remembrance
questioning
trust
indiv – rem indiv good times
gp – comm hx
indiv – hope expressed
gp – God asked directly – arguing with God
urge God to be God
– not our fault, bitterness

Then compare what you discover with my notes in the margin of page 16.

The parts of prayer

These two Psalms illustrate the features that may be expected to appear in our prayers.

Some addressing of God: as God, living God, sovereign, my rock, my stronghold, my king, my God. Addressing someone presupposes that there is someone there. Prayer is different from reflection. It is part of a relationship with another person.

Some expression of feelings and relating of experiences. There are three forms of expression which often appear.

- I may speak of how 'I' feel.
- I may speak of what 'they' have done – the way other people have been treating me.
- I may speak of what 'you' (God) have done or failed to do.

This section, in which the psalmist laments the suffering of individuals or of the whole people, is usually the most substantial element in the psalm. The focus of the psalm is usually on telling God about the situation.

Some expression of trust and hope which the psalmist is still committed to, despite everything.

Some actual request, asking God to do something. This element is usually rather brief compared with what we usually say in *our* prayers. It is not very specific, characteristically asking simply for God to turn, to act, and to punish enemies.

A promise: to give God the glory for answering this prayer, and to join in the ongoing praise of the people of God.

Anger in prayer

Anger and prayer may not seem to you to go together very well. In the Psalms they belong naturally together. There are at least two reasons for this.

God's anger
Sometimes a psalm commits itself to sharing God's anger at the wrong there is in the world. Thus in Psalm 139:21-24 ☛ we commit ourselves (with the appropriate negative feeling and commitment) to hate people who have a committed hatred for God. We then invite God to test whether we really mean that commitment.

The Psalms assume that prayer is not something which belongs only in our individual private lives. It is part of life as a whole, and part of the fulfilment of God's purpose in the world. It thus reflects God's own nature and concerns, and in particular God's commitment to reigning in the world with fairness and in peace. Our anger is part of the image of God in us, a creative energy designed to contribute to the fulfilment of God's purpose. Prayer is one of the contexts in which we can exercise it positively.

Our anger
Sometimes a psalm is working on the assumption that God shares (or should share) *our* anger at wrong done to us. Notoriously Psalm 137 declares the happiness of Babylon's punishers, because they will dash her children against the rocks.

Whatever the rights and wrongs of Israel's feelings, the Psalms assume that negative feelings can be expressed to God in prayer. The Psalms do not expect us to express to God only the feelings that we *should* have, but the feelings we *do* have. We do not have to hide our angry feelings from God – God can handle them. Perhaps it is assumed that it is better for us to express them to God than to bottle them up – otherwise they may be displaced into other forms of expression, or we will work them out inappropriately on the objects of our anger.

O Lord, how I hate those who hate you!
How I despise those who rebel against you!
I hate them with a total hatred;
I regard them as my enemies.
Examine me, O God, and know my mind;
test me, and discover my thoughts.
Find out if there is any evil in me,
and guide me in the everlasting way.

BAD FEELING?

'Hatred' in the Bible is more a matter of commitment than of the emotions. So is 'love'.

Prayer is one of the safest places to express anger.

THE EXPERIENCE OF PRAISE

The praise of the Psalms comes in two main forms:

Worship or adoration
Sometimes the Psalms are giving themselves to praise because of things that *are always true* – aspects of God's character or things God has done in the past to make us His people.

Thanksgiving or testimony
Sometimes the Psalms are giving themselves to praise because of things that *have been true just for the person praising* – like the experience of God's deliverance or healing in a personal situation.

How to worship

The nature of a worship psalm is illustrated in a nutsnell by Psalm 117. There are two features: a challenge to worship, and the reasons for worship:

1 *Praise Yahweh, all you nations*
Extol him, all you peoples
2 *For great is his love towards us*
The faithfulness of Yahweh
endures for ever

The challenge may be a bidding to Israel to worship, or a challenge to all the world, or a commitment on the part of the individual or the community. Psalm 150 comprises nothing but this challenge.

Psalm 96 illustrates the two sides to this expression of worship. Both are bodily. On the one side, it is loud and resounding, jubilant and enthusiastic, offered with hands raised or clapping, feet stamping or dancing. On the other, it involves trembling and bowing, self–lowering and prostration – not the genteel kneeling of a traditional British church, but the lowering of the whole person, still practised in prayer today by Muslims. When the Bible translations use words such as 'worship', these are body–words, words for prostration.

The challenge to praise is normally buttressed by reasons. The word 'for' is the key to a worship psalm. The worship it expresses is not mindless enthusiasm or mindless self-humbling, but a logical, enthusiastic and humble response to the facts about God. In Psalm 96 these facts are God's greatness, creative power, unique holiness, authoritative sovereignty in the world – and the certainty that God will implement that sovereignty in the world and reign in true justice. Such facts are reason both for jubilant enthusiasm and awed prostration.

If we want to learn how to praise God, Psalms such as these point us in two directions:

- they invite us to come out of our heads and into our bodies. Worship is not something that

PSALMS AND US

Answers from page 14

- There is a great freedom and frankness in telling God exactly how things are – in being open with God (and thus with ourselves) about a sense of pain or loss.
- There is considerable stress in the Psalms on 'remembering'. They spend a lot of time reminding God (and themselves) of how good things used to be. There is a kind of 'owning' of what has been going on rather than hiding from it, and a pressing of God to make the future more like the past.
- To judge from Psalm 44, an important element in prayer is arguing with God. The reminding is all part of that argument.
- To judge from Psalms 42-43, a significant element in prayer is arguing with oneself. Talking with God reminds us that God opens up possibilities for the future.
- The Psalms are bold in confronting God. They have no hesitation in accusing God of having forgotten us or of being asleep.
- The Psalms urge God to be God: to be the rock, stronghold, the steadfastly-committed one that God is supposed to be.
- To judge from Psalm 44, in order to pray this way there has to be no obstacle between us and God on our side. Either we have to forsake wrongdoing, or we have to be able to say that God's abandoning of us is not our fault.

belongs in quietness or in the heart. To be true worship it requires noise and expression.

- they invite us to remind ourselves who God is and what God has done. Awareness of that should drive us to that enthusiasm and awe.

Study Psalms 95 and 81. How far do they confirm what we have been seeing in Psalm 96? What do they add?

When circumstances lower our eyes and we can no longer see any reason for worship, the Psalms exist to remind us what worship involves and to set a new song on our lips. They have the capacity to draw us out of our understandable preoccupation with the problems and the difficulties of the day – not so that we pretend that these do not exist, but so that we have something else to put alongside them.

The psalms portray an alternative world to the one which confronts our eyes. They invite us to believe that this alternative world in which God reigns is actually the real world. When we have become convinced of that possibility again, we may be able to go out into the world which confronts our eyes and live in it in the conviction that it is not so real – and it may become less real.

How to be grateful

The other aspect of praise has a more personal dynamic. Suppose you have been overwhelmed by depression, attacked by enemies or abandoned by God – or all three. Then you have been released, delivered, and newly-loved. That experience drives you into a different kind of praise, one which relates to your personal experience of God's involvement in your own life.

Psalm 116 provides an example. Like much thanksgiving, it works backwards. It recalls Brian Wren's hymn *Sing my song backwards*, which speaks of the difference in the way we view the story of Jesus' life (and death) when we look at them in the light of his resurrection. The psalm recollects the trouble of the recent past from the perspective of God's deliverance.

You can turn Psalm 116 back into the story of what happened, in the order in which it happened ☛

The psalm itself does not come in this logical order – and shows that our heart-felt response to God does not work in that logical way! But the psalm shows us how thanksgiving speaks of:

- my **past** hurt and prayer and experience of God's intervention
- my **present** response
- my **future** commitments

Worship or thanks?

Giving thanks for God's goodness to *me* in particular is not a better way of praising than offering worship for what God always is. It's not a worse way either. Both form part of the normal life of praise as the Psalms portray it. They feed each other.

- What we acknowledge in worship supports the prayer we pray in times of need, and thus leads towards the thanksgiving we eventually offer for God's intervention.

- When we experience God's intervention, it proves once more the truth of what we say in worship, so that thanksgiving naturally leads into renewed worship.

Which kind of praise do you find it more natural to offer to God? Can you find ways of allowing it to lead you into the other?

PSALM 116

- I was overwhelmed by trouble, as if by death itself (v. 3, 6)
- I was dismayed at the way everyone let me down (v. 11)
- I knew I was straight in my relationship with God (v. 6)
- I still believed in God (v. 10)
- I called out, 'Save me!' (v. 4)
- God listened (v. 1–2)
- God rescued me from my deathly sadness (v. 6, 7, 8, 16)
- I come to worship to make my costly response to God's goodness to me (v. 12–14, 17–18)
- I give my public testimony to God's love and justice (v. 5, 15, 18–19)
- I love God the more because of this experience (v. 1)
- I can walk before God in the land of the living now (v. 9)
- I can tell myself to rest in God for the future (v. 7)
- I know I can always call on God like that in the future (v. 2)

A TEST OF SPIRITUALITY

The book of Job revolves around the story of a man who has everything, but who loses it all in a series of catastrophes. It recalls the way people tried to help him cope with this experience, and the way he actually coped.

Job is not an attempt to answer the question 'Why do people suffer?' (or if it is, it is a spectacular failure). It offers insights on how to cope with suffering – which is a different question.

But for our present purpose it has another significance. In the story of Job (and perhaps in everyone's experience of loss and grief), suffering raises questions about how Job lived with God – about Job's spirituality, if you like. It raises questions about the basis of Job's relationship with God (and the basis of anyone's relationship with God).

A commitment questioned

Behind the story of Job's loss is a scene in the heavenly 'cabinet', where decisions get taken about matters on earth. One of God's presidential *aides* is called 'the Adversary' (the Hebrew word is *satan*, but it is misleading to equate this person with 'Satan' in the New Testament). Apparently the Adversary's task is to make sure that justice gets done on earth and to make sure no-one gets away with things they ought not to get away with. It is his task to be suspicious. (You can probably think of someone you know who is like that...)

In Job's day, there was no-one more godly than Job. The Adversary raises the question whether Job is godly only for what he gets out of it. And perhaps God is colluding with Job, enjoying the worship and commitment of a man such as him. For each of them, religion is then a matter of 'You scratch my back and I'll scratch yours.' The Adversary therefore proposes that the blessings Job enjoys should be withdrawn, so that it can be established whether his godliness will also disappear.

An essential question about living with God is, 'Do I worship God because God is God, or for what I get out of it?'

You may well feel that what God allows to happen to Job in order to discover the answer to this question, is immoral. I think that this is a fictional story, and to me that makes a difference. But even if it isn't, we have abundant evidence from elsewhere in the Bible that God does test people to see whether their trust and commitment are real. The assumption that underlies this is that there is no other way for God to know – or at least that there is no other way for it to be publicly established.

God gives us the chance to show who we are. God does not rely on computer projections. That has exciting implications for living with God.

Brutal honesty with God

A dominant feature of the story of Job is a series of extraordinarily frank prayers which Job prays. In our terms 'prayers' may hardly seem the right word for them, dominated as they are by curses, questions, objections, wishes, insults, complaints and challenges.

We have seen that the prayers of the Psalms are characterized by a frankness of this kind, on a much smaller scale. Job's assaults on God are those prayers taken to the extreme. They show more powerfully than anything else in Scripture that there is no limit to what we can say to God. And the ultimate compliment which God pays this verbal terrorist, is to say that he has spoken what is right about God (42:8).

Suffering is our teacher

Despite the seriousness of the story of Job, the contribution of his three 'friends' Eliphaz, Bildad and Zophar, and their youthful associate Elihu, make us smile. The three arrive to grieve with Job and comfort him in his loss. For a week they simply sit silently with him like a Jewish family sitting *shiva* with a bereaved person. It is the best thing they ever do. Once they open their mouths, they never take their feet out of them.

It seems that they can cope with Job as long as he suffers silently, but not when he says what he is thinking. Like most of us, they believe in a world where God blesses those who live by trust, worship and obedience. Job's experience, and then his words, place a question mark by the reality of that world.

Their understandable reaction is to reassert that the world is just like that – how could it be otherwise? They do so on the basis of tradition, spiritual experience and reason – three vital handmaids of a pastor or spiritual director. All that they say about the character of God and the way God relates to us is true. The trouble is, it does not apply to Job at this moment. That strange beginning to the book of Job told us that Job is in fact a special case. But they have to make Job fit their theology, and are prepared to rewrite Job's life to turn him into a secret sinner, rather than rethink that theology.

When Elihu appears, behind all the bluster he does have something distinctive to say. His point is that loss can be not so much God's punishment for our sin, as God's way of drawing us back. Suffering is designed to teach us spiritual lessons. The irony of Elihu's contribution is that this is now a standard 'Christian' approach to the question of suffering. But it is only one staging-post in the book's argument.

Beyond our understanding

It has been suggested that the nearest Hebrew word there is to 'spirituality' is the word 'wisdom'. Just before Job's final speech there is a poem about wisdom. It is printed as if it were part of Job's words, but it is more like an independent poem commenting on the debate and anticipating God's words. For us there is some significance in the question it asks: 'Where then does wisdom come from?' (28:12). God alone knows the way to it. If there is anything we can say about finding it, it is that worship of God and avoidance of evil are the keys (28:28).

When God appears to Job, it is not to answer questions but to ask them – and aggressively, in Job's own fashion (chapters 38-41). If God's words can be summarized, they have two thrusts:

- The world is much bigger than Job. If Job is in the wrong, it is not in anything he has done, but in his expectation that he ought to be able to understand everything. After two long chapters Job is prepared to admit defeat.
- If Job is such an expert, does he think that he can make a better job of keeping the world in order than God has? Job has to learn to submit to God and to trust God, even where he cannot understand.

The great irony of this speech is that, whereas there was a perfectly straightforward answer to the question of what had been happening to Job, he is never given it. God's speeches bear no relationship to the *reasons* for Job's experience. One of the delights of that is that it shows Job living the same way as we do. It reminds us of the possibility that the enigmas of our lives may after all have answers.

JOB

HAPPILY EVER AFTER?

Many people wish that the story of Job did not have its 'artificially' happy ending. For me the promise that life will have a happy ending is important. In the end God is fair and God does care about us.

THE CHILD OF GOD

The story of Jesus' ministry is flanked by two accounts of God's dealings with him and his dealings with God. The first happens in the harsh sunlight of the deep broad Jordan Valley. The second takes place in the steep narrow cleft of the Kidron Valley, in the darkness of late evening. They are his baptism and Gethsemane.

Four aspects of these dealings between Jesus and God recur:

The demands of childhood

As Jesus is baptized, a cleft appears in the skies themselves and a dove comes to rest on Jesus. To judge from Genesis 8, the dove is the symbol of creativity and the future, rather than the symbol of peace. This fits Matthew's explanation that it stands for the spirit of God. And a voice from the sky says, 'This is my son, my beloved; with him I am well-pleased'.

God's voice puts together phrases from three different biblical passages.

- The first (from Psalm 2:7) explicitly identifies Jesus as God's son and implicitly promises him a share in God's glory.
- The second (from Genesis 22:2) puts God and Jesus in the same position as Abraham and Isaac when Isaac is about to be offered as a sacrifice – which is a more worrying proposition.
- The third (from Isaiah 42:1) makes Jesus also God's servant, who will have to sacrifice himself before bringing freedom to Israel and to the world.

In Gethsemane, Jesus prays, 'My Father, if it be possible, may this cup be taken from me.' The cup is the cup of poison which those same chapters of Isaiah spoke of. 'Yet not as I will, but as you will'.

To be able to relate to God as Father is a huge privilege, but it also makes huge demands.

Being stretched

After meeting with God, Jesus is driven away from the crowds into the desert, driven by the Spirit who had come to rest on him, to be tested by the devil. He presents Jesus with ideas of varying plausibility. 'When you are hungry, why not use your resources to meet your needs? After all, you need to look after yourself. Do something spectacular, take risks, God has promised to look after you. Your job is to rule the world and the world belongs to me; bow down to me and you *will* rule the world.'

God does not tempt, but God does test – and the joke is that the Greek word is the same. When you go through such experiences, God wishes to *stretch* you through them, but the evil one wishes to *trip* you through them.

In Luke's version, after these temptations the devil left Jesus 'for a while'. When did the 'while' end? It is certainly the case that stretching is going on in Gethsemane, stretching almost to breaking point as Jesus is 'overwhelmed' by what he is going through. Jesus reached maturity through what he suffered (Hebrews 5:7-9), as we must do.

Submitting to God

In the desert, Jesus answers each of the devil's suggestions with an 'It is written', referring himself (and us and the devil) to insights from the Scriptures that related to them.

- It is God's decision that fixes whether we live or die.
- It is my task to trust God, not to test God.
- Denying God's 'godness' is no way to win the world for God.

Those replies came from the Scriptures. Since he had first heard them read when he sat on Joseph's or Mary's knee, he had been absorbing them and letting himself be shaped by them. It had all been a preparation for this moment.

In Gethsemane there is no word of Scripture to cover what is going on. Sometimes we are in the fortunate position that Scripture clearly covers what is set in front of us; the only questions are whether we know the relevant Scriptures and whether we will take any notice of them. On other occasions we are on our own with God with some aspect of our lives, and the question is simply whether we will let ourselves hear what God says – whether we are willing to say, 'My Father, if it is not possible for this cup to be taken away unless I drink it, may your will be done.'

Our heavenly provider

'Then the devil left him, and angels came and attended him.' I wonder what the devil and the angels looked like? Whenever angels appear in Scripture, they look like human beings (which opens up the possibility of our entertaining angels unawares). When Satan tempts Jesus at Caesarea Philippi, he does it by using Peter. Satan is too clever to go around looking like Satan.

Most of our experiences of the angelic and the demonic come through people. Perhaps it was so in the desert.. Jesus has said 'No' to making his own bread because he knows that whether or not you have bread is not what finally decides whether you live. The point is now proved, as God sees that he gets cared for when he does not take care for himself.

In Luke's Gethsemane story, likewise, an angel is there to strengthen him. We are not left to cope with such experiences on our own.

THE LORD'S PRAYER

The Lord's Prayer is a prayer Jesus teaches, but it also looks like a prayer he prayed.

- We too are invited to pray to God as father, and acknowledge the demand of that ('hallowed be...').
- We too are invited to be stretched, and pray not to be overstretched ('lead us not...').
- We are invited to offer the same submission as he offered ('your will be done').
- We are invited to seek the same provision he received ('give us today...').
- We are invited to seek forgiveness. He needed no forgiveness for himself, but the story of his baptism shows how he identified with us in *our* need of it.

CHRIST AT THE CENTRE

Paul often finds reason to talk about his relationship with God and his prayers; 2 Corinthians, for example, is a rich source for understanding how he coped with pressure. But it is Philippians that gives us a systematic and reflective account of how Paul saw his life with God.

The past is junk

We gain some of our sense of who we are and whether we matter from where we came from and what we have achieved.

I am proud of coming from Birmingham, of going to its best school, of getting a First Class degree from Oxford University, of being accepted for training for the Church of England ministry, of being invited to teach in a theological college, of gaining a PhD, of writing books, of being awarded a DD, of being appointed a senior Professor in a big seminary in the USA. I learn from Paul that such pride is folly. He knows that it is all junk (see Philippians 3:4-9).

Paul was a man who had everything. He had all the grounds there could be for human confidence.

- He was circumcised on the eighth day: so God's promise to Abraham belonged to him.
- He belonged to the people of Israel, the line of Isaac rather than Ishmael, Jacob rather than Esau.
- He belonged to the tribe of Benjamin: he knew his ancestry within Israel, and he identified with the small but central tribe which produced Israel's first king.
- He was a Hebrew–speaking Jew, not one who could not be at home in his ancestral language.
- He was a Pharisee, the group who were most committed to putting God's word into practice in their lives.
- He felt such keen zeal for God's purpose that he had harried the people who seemed to be leading Israel astray by claiming that Jesus was messiah.
- He could stand before God confident that he really had lived his life in obedience to God's written word.

Until Christ knocked him over on his way across the Golan Heights, Paul had absolute confidence in his religious commitment – the same kind of confidence that we see him having later in the truth of the gospel. But Christ *did* knock him over, and he saw that the crucified Jesus was actually the messiah. He found himself in touch with God in a new way.

This new touch from God did not stem from *his* commitment to God's word, but from *Jesus*' commitment to him, which had obviously got nothing to do with anything he had done for Jesus. His eyes were opened, metaphorically as well as physically. He realized that what God had now done for him made everything he had had before relatively worthless. The word he uses to describe it is much less polite than the NIV's word 'rubbish'.

The present is Christ

You probably know people about whom you might say, 'His life *is* football' or 'For her, life *is* her children.' It's the thing which makes life worth living, the thing for which we would give anything up, the thing which animates us – and which enables us to go to sleep contented.

In talking about the present, Paul reflects out loud on what he really wants (see Philippians 1:21-26). 'I rather fancy the idea of dying, because that means to go and be with Christ, but for the sake of people like you Philippians (who perhaps found him a bit insufferable) I am prepared to stay in this life for a while. Either way, to me, to live *is* Christ.'

Working for Christ was what gave Paul his 'buzz'. That could be a form of workaholism. But if he really means that he would actually prefer to die and to be with Christ, then the preserving of that desire perhaps acted as a safety mechanism against being a workaholic for Christ.

Paul keeps using the word 'joy' in this letter (see especially 4:4-7) – and the joy is in the person of Christ, not just in the activity done for Christ's sake. Interestingly, when Paul talks directly about himself, he speaks not of joy but of contentment (4:12-13). He has learned to live with little as well as with much because, for him, life *is* Christ.

The future is...

I talked earlier (on page 2) about my subconscious assumption as a young man that I had 'arrived' as a human being. I was not proud of the fact; indeed, I was a bit sad. There was nothing else to happen. But in fact, as years have passed, I have picked up speed. (When you are over the hill, you do pick up speed...)

You might have assumed that Paul thought he had arrived – twice really. He first thought he had arrived as a committed Pharisee, and now he seemed to have arrived as a committed Christian. Actually he is still someone on the move, on a journey, running a race (Philippians 3:10-14).

- He wants to know Christ! Apparently he does not.
- He wants to know the power of Christ's resurrection! Apparently he does not.
- Then he speaks of coming to share in Christ's sufferings – which is odd, because how does death follow on resurrection?

Indeed it does so. The order is set out in the story of his confrontation by Christ on the Damascus Road (see Acts 9). First he acknowledges the risen Jesus. Then he is to discover how much he is to suffer for Christ's sake. Going from resurrection to suffering, he will in due course find his own resurrection (Philippians 3:10-11).

Paul is pressing on towards a target. It could easily be a form of Christian 'justification by works'. Perhaps when he speaks of pressing on to take hold of that for which Christ takes hold of him, he is reminding himself of something. He has already urged his readers to work out their salvation on the basis of the fact that God is working in them. He can be confident for them (and for himself) because God started this process and is involved with it. But he also expects them to be apprehensive (2:12), and he wants to take nothing for granted himself (3:11-14). Everything also depends on them (and him) carrying on to the end of the course.

FRANCES HAVERGAL

(1836-1879)

Frances Ridley Havergal was the daughter of a parish clergyman who was himself musical, and she wrote and composed hymns from an early age. She wrote quickly as ideas and words flashed upon her; her hymns were born 'full-grown'. 'Writing is praying with me... He would give me, not merely thoughts and power, but also every word'. She was ill for much of her life and died in her 40s in the midst of an active ministry among the poor in South Wales. Her best-known hymn is *Take My Life*: and the following is an excerpt from a meditation/commentary on it called *Kept For the Master's Use*. She does not seem to notice that she is subverting her own hymn-writing, though she may imply that her own hymns were not self-consciously written as 'sacred song'.

A great many so-called 'sacred songs' are so plaintive and pathetic that they help to give a gloomy idea of religion. Now *don't* sing these; come out boldly, and sing definitely and unmistakably for your King, and of your King, and to your King. You will soon find, and even outsiders will have to own, that it is a *good* thing thus to show forth His loving-kindness and His faithfulness (see Ps. xcii.1-3).

Only one thing I would add: I believe there is nothing like singing His own words. The preacher claims the promise, 'My word shall not return unto Me void,' and why should not the singer equally claim it? Why should we use His own inspired words, with faith in their power, when speaking or writing, and content ourselves with human words put into rhyme (and sometimes very feeble rhyme) for our singing?

What a vista of happy work opens out here! What is there to prevent our using this mightiest of all agencies committed to human agents, the word is quick and powerful, and sharper than any two-edged sword, whenever we are asked to sing? By this means even a young girl may be privileged to make that word sound in the ears of many who would not listen to it otherwise. By this the incorruptible seed may be sown in otherwise unreachable ground.

But there is much more than this. One feels the power of His words for one's self as one sings. One loves them and rejoices in them, and what can be greater help to any singer than that? And one knows they are true, and that they cannot really return void, and what can give greater confidence than that? God *may* bless the singing of any words, but he *must* bless the singing of His own word, if that promise means what it says!

The only real difficulty in the matter is that Scripture songs, as a rule, require a little more practice than others. Then practise them a little more! You think nothing of the trouble of learning, for instance, a sonata, which takes you many a good hour's practice before you can render it perfectly and expressively. But you shrink from a song, the accompaniment of which you cannot read off without any trouble at all. And you never think of such a thing as taking one tenth the pains to learn that accompaniment that you took to learn that sonata! Very liekly, too, you take the additional pains to learn the sonata off by heart, so that you may it more effectively. But you do not take pains to learn your accompaniment by heart, so that you may throw all your power into the expression of the words, undistracted by reading the notes and turning over the leaves. If is far more useful to have half a dozen Scripture songs thoroughly learnt and made your own, than to have in your portfolios several dozen easy settings of sacred poetry which you get through with your eyes fixed on the notes. And every one thus thoroughly mastered makes it easier to master others.

You will say that all this refers only to drawing-room singing. So it does, primarily, but then it is the drawing-room singing which has been so little for Jesus and so much for self and society; and so much less has been said about it, and so much less *done*. There would not be half the complaints of the difficulty of witnessing for Christ in even professedly Christian homes and circles, if every converted singer were also a consecrated one. For nothing raises or lowers the tone of a whole evening so much as the character of the music. There are few things which show more clearly that, as a rule, a very definite step in advance is needed beyond being a believer or even a worker for Christ. Over how many grand or cottage pianos could the Irish Society's motto, 'For Jesus' sake *only*.' be hung, without being either a frequent reproach or altogether inappropriate.

REVIEW

Scripture is the ultimate source from which to review your life with God. Look back through *two* of the topics in this Unit, and review parts of your life with God in the light of them. How would you like to begin living your life with God differently?

Write two reflections (one for each topic you review), so your thoughts don't just get lost. You will find it helpful to be able to come back to these reflections later.

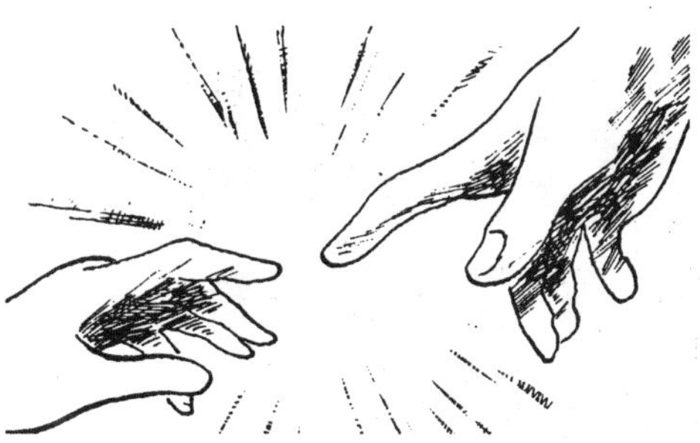

Unit 3

BACK TO BASICS

PURPOSE

This Unit outlines four key chapters in Paul's letter to the Romans, which expound the basics of Christian experience.

All the religious wisdom and spiritual techniques in the world will not draw us closer to God unless our foundation in God is solid. Here is an opportunity to re-examine your foundations before you build more on them.

CONTENTS

CONFIDENT AT HEART?

Read Romans 5:1-11, as you study these pages. Make notes on particular things you learn; use the box on page 36.

What is 'living with God' supposed to be like? The best word to summarize the characteristics which Paul describes in Romans 5:1-11 is *confidence*. The Christian life is not supposed to be characterized by insecurity, anxiety, worry, uncertainty, hesitation or fear.

Confidence about the past

In Philippians Paul tells us how he once had a confidence about the past, but threw this confidence away (see page 22). Here he looks at his past in a different way – how *bad* it was. Maybe it's only when you realize that you have been scooped out of the mire by Christ, that you can analyse your former situation and see that it *was* mire. What we were is:

- **ungodly**: people who refused to treat God as God.
- **sinners**: failures who couldn't live up to our own standards, let alone God's.
- **enemies**: there was a state of conflict between God and us, even if we didn't realize it.
- **helpless**: we couldn't do anything about all that.

Modern Christians may not like that kind of analysis:

- We see ourselves as needy and hurt, needing healing and renewal, not as sinners needing forgiveness.
- We are trying to accept ourselves as we are, to love ourselves as we love our neighbour, not to be negative about ourselves.
- We are aware of suffering in the world, and worry more about how *God* can be just than about how *we* can be.
- We have learned to be positive about the world and the body, so talk of 'the world, the flesh, and the devil' can seem rather quaint.

We need to see the negative side to our past if we are to understand the cross and have the confidence we want. Obviously confidence about our past is the last thing we are entitled to have, if we are ungodly, sinners, enemies and helpless. But those facts are only the *backdrop* to the gospel. Set alongside the facts about *our* past are the facts about *his* past. Our confidence about the past is based on what God has done for us in Christ.

That is what 'justification by faith' means. Christ has died for us, and we can face the facts about *our* past on the basis of the facts about *his*. In the development of your life with God, there may be nothing more important than the realization that you are justified by faith. It is the key to everything. This is where you have to start, because other confidences are built on it.

Confidence with God

Confidence about the past results in confidence in God's presence. The first word of Romans 5 is the word 'therefore'. The Christian life is based not just on feelings or on experiences but on logic. We can confidently come into God's presence because of what Christ has done for us.

We then 'stand in grace'. Grace means someone is well-disposed towards us. When we have done something wrong to someone, we know what it is like to feel they are *not* well-disposed towards us. There is resentment or frostiness. Then they are cheery and give you a hug, and you know that you stand in grace. (Of course, sometimes they may be frosty for other reasons, and maybe we just shrug our shoulders and wait till they get out of their sulk...)

Standing in grace is a fact of the gospel. It's not like putting your money in the fruit machine – sometimes you get three tangerines, which means you have had a good experience of God, but sometimes you get nothing. Whether I can be confident in the presence of God isn't decided by my fickle emotions, or by God's. It's decided by the *fact* that Christ died for me. I can confidently be aware of the presence of God at any moment. In a quiet or noisy place, at any time, I can talk to God the way I talk to a lover or a friend.

There are two opposite dangers which may threaten our confidence in God's presence:

- **A superficial confidence**, a matey confidence. It is an awesome fact that we have access to God's presence – and it's only because Christ died for us.
- **A lack of confidence** about being able to enter God's presence. We may desire to meet God but be uncertain about how to do so. For some people that's why they're interested in spirituality – they are trying to discover *how* to get in touch with God. But being welcomed into the presence of God and having confidence about your place there, are questions of theology and the gospel, before they are questions of method. Focusing on spiritual method without having your confidence grounded in Christ, is like reading sex-manuals before you have established a loving relationship.

If you're not sure whether God is accessible to you, and not sure whether you can go through the motions of prayer, you need to remind yourself about the nature of the gospel, about that confidence in entering the presence of God which Christ's death for you gives.

Confidence about the future

As Christians we rejoice in our hope of sharing the glory of God. We will be saved from the wrath of God. As with sin, modern Christians no longer take God's judgment very seriously. But like Jesus, Paul sees God's wrath hanging over the people of God.

It is in that context that we rejoice in a hope of sharing God's glory. The future turns out to be a choice between wrath and glory. I have the prospect of seeing the shining brightness of God's person. It's still a hope for the future, but because of our confidence in that future, we rejoice in that hope now and already begin to be transformed by that hope in the present.

Confidence in trouble

We live in hope (v. 2) which does not disappoint us (v. 5) – and so we experience some fulfilment even now.

Strangely, it happens through our suffering, through what pressure and hardship do to us and where they drive us. So we even rejoice in the sufferings themselves because of what they do (v. 3). All the evidence is that pressure and stress are built into God's purpose for us, because they mean that we prove ourselves and prove God, which in turn increases our confidence in God and in the future.

When we feel most under pressure, that can be when God makes us most aware of His love, poured into our hearts through the Holy Spirit. The awareness of God's love offers further proof that our confidence is justified.

IN THE WAY OF LOVE

How do I put myself in the way of that love? It is God's gift, so:

- I have to let the giver control the giving of the gift. It doesn't depend on what I deserve but on how God sees my need.
- I can ask the giver for it, ask to be overwhelmed by God's love. 'How much more will God give his Holy Spirit to those who ask.' (Luke 11:13)
- I need to look at the means by which God gives it. This relates to our confidence about the past. As we contemplate the cross, the ultimate expression of that love, the Holy Spirit may overwhelm us with an awareness of it.

STARTING LIFE OVER

Read Romans 6:1-14 as you study these pages. Make notes on particular things you learn; use the box on page 36.

The trouble is, confidence can lead to carelessness, slackness and irresponsibility. 'Let's relax and do nothing. I don't have to worry about my sin and my guilt – God has forgiven me and will continue to forgive me. That really proves that *God* is my confidence.'

If I had been Paul responding to that suggestion, I might have said, 'Aha, if you take that attitude, you may find that God does not forgive you.' That isn't what Paul says. He lets his talk about a Christian's confidence stand, stark and scandalous. Yes, he really means that being right with God depends solely on what God has done and not at all on anything I do. The only thing I contributed to my salvation was my sin. Whether I serve God, love God, pray to God, or give God everything I have, it still contributes nothing to my salvation.

So if I don't begin to live a different life, what happens? What Paul says is not that I then get thrown out of the kingdom, but that talk of that kind proves that I haven't understood what happened to me. Otherwise I wouldn't talk that way.

'We died to sin. How can we live in it any longer?'

Paul goes on to explain that enigmatic statement. It's a logical step-by-step argument.

Step 1

(v. 3a): 'You've been baptized, haven't you?' That set the seal on a relationship between me and Christ. I was baptized into Christ, into a relationship with Christ. There was a point when God reached out to me. If I was too small to know what was going on, that makes the miracle of that even more terrific. (OK, so I'm not a Baptist…)

Step 2

(v. 3b): What went on at our baptism? 'We were baptized into a relationship with his death. We were therefore buried with him through baptism into death'.

Christ died, was buried, lay dead. Those are facts. Now, says Paul, when you were baptized, that means that (just as factually) you died with Christ, you were buried with Christ, you lay dead with Christ. If someone does something as your representative, in effect *you've* done it. It happens with sport, in wars and in parliament. What our representatives do, in effect we do. So, as Paul puts it elsewhere, if one person died on behalf of everybody, in effect everybody died.

Of course one person's actions don't automatically affect everyone – only if that person is *their* representative. My Member of Parliament represents me (and a few others…), but she doesn't represent you – unless you come and live quite near me, then she will. It even works backwards. Things done by my MP for our area in the past, become things done for you if you come here.

Step 3

(v. 4-5): For Christ, death wasn't the end, and neither is it for those he represents. Christ died, and Christ rose to new life. Baptism means that in effect you died at Calvary, and it also means that you came back from the dead.

Step 4

(v. 6-7): This death (Christ's and ours) is a death to sin. Christ died to sin at Calvary; therefore in effect you also died to sin there and are now dead to sin (see v. 10a, 11a).

In what sense did Christ die to sin? He chose to live in the realm of sin, to be treated as someone whom sin could control, and was willing to pay the legal penalty for that. But once you've paid a penalty for something, you're a free person. The law has no more claim on you, so the realm of sin (which operates by means of law) has lost control of you. That's what 'Christ died to sin on the cross' means. He let sin control him, let the law exact its penalty, and once he had done that, he was free of it.

He did all that as our representative. He paid sin's penalty on our behalf. So because he died to sin, in effect we died to sin. Sin has no more power over *us* because its penalty has been paid in Christ. 'A dead man is no longer answerable for his sin' (v. 7, NEB). And we are dead people. Sin no longer has any rights over us.

Step 5

(v. 8-11): After dying to sin, Christ could live to God. Because we have died to sin in Christ, *we* can live to God too. His resurrection means we too start a new life, no longer slaves to sin but free to serve God. Indeed, we can't really do anything else – that is Paul's point in the whole chapter. It's not a moral point about something that you *should* do, but a logical point. It's not guilt-news, it's good news...

Step 6

(v. 11): Now you've come to look at yourself as someone who really has gone through death and resurrection, you need to consider yourself in that light, view yourself as dead to sin and alive to God.

Sometimes people have talked about this 'reckoning' as if it involved reckoning something was the case when it wasn't, with a view to making it true. 'I'm not actually dead to sin yet, but if I reckon I am, I will find that I am.' That's not Paul's argument here.

When we say someone is 'dead to the world', the things around have no impact on them. So 'dead to sin' can sound as if it means sin doesn't

have any impact on us; we can't feel its tug.

That isn't what Paul means. Being dead to sin means having paid sin's penalty. Paul doesn't say we *ought* to be dead to sin. He says we *are*, because Christ died for us. He doesn't say we are dying to sin. He says we *have* died – it was once-for-all. He wants us to regard ourselves in the light of the actual fact that we *are* dead to sin, that sin has no right to lord it over us because we have paid its penalty. Instead we are alive to God, and free to live.

FACTS AND FEELINGS

I knew a woman whose mother dominated her as if she was a girl of 10. She would get into a stew about having to phone her mother, knowing the trouble she would find herself in for one reason or another. Her mother had a mysterious power over her that reduced her to a little girl again. How is she to make progress as a person? It has to be by starting to live in relation to her mother in accordance with the *facts* – she is grown up and independent – and not in accordance with the *fantasy* that her mother continues to con her with. She has to regard herself as grown-up – which she is.

That is how we are in relation to sin. Sin treats us the same way it treats everyone else: beguiling, threatening, tempting. It doesn't acknowledge that we've paid its penalty in Christ, that we're dead to it. We allow its bluff to work. We fall for its temptations. We start to live in a legal way again, seeing ourselves as guilty and unworthy. We're pulled back into a cycle of failure, guilt and more self-centredness. And it is then tempting to infer that we are not dead to sin. Dying to sin, perhaps; ought to die to sin, no doubt; but dead to sin, definitely not.

That is wrong. When that woman panics at her mother's voice on the phone, it doesn't prove she's only a little girl after all. She *is* a woman. The trouble is that the little-girl-self inside her hasn't yet surrendered its power. If she is to make progress as a human being, she has to count herself a woman, regard herself as an adult. So it is with us and sin, even when 'being dead to sin' is not how it feels.

Step 7

(v. 12-14): God's part has been done – we have in effect died and been raised. We must therefore give ourselves to God, and let God reign in our life. We *can* now do that as we could not before, and we can live in accordance with facts and not fantasy – because we are not under law, we are under grace.

FORGET THE RULES!

Read Romans 7:1-25 as you study these pages. Make notes on particular things you learn; use the box on page 36.

As Christians, the law can't 'get' us any more, and we now live by grace. So why bother with the law – or with rules of any kind? The law existed to guide us to live in a moral way. If Paul is telling us that the law doesn't apply to us now, isn't he encouraging immorality, just 'doing what you like'?

On the contrary, says Paul. Now that people are free from God's law in Christ, they can actually *do* what God's law says. Just because you tell people that they are free from the law, doesn't mean you are encouraging them to sin.

Paul expresses his basic point in one sentence in verses 5-6. There are three snapshots from the life of a Christian:

- First, we are living under the law, on the way to death.
- Second, we are discharged from our bondage, and die to it.
- Third, we are serving God in the new life of the Spirit.

Frame 1: Living by the book

To start with, we were living with the law, and therefore on the way to death. That doesn't mean the law itself is bad (the law was written by the best-selling author of all time…). It just means that being told what to do doesn't make you do it. God's commands are holy, but they can't bring you a life of holiness. Indeed, they often have the opposite effect – sin and therefore death.

There are two mistakes we can make about politics. One is to underestimate its importance. The other is to overestimate it. For all the importance of politics, there are severe limitations to what political involvement and social reform will achieve. It will not bring in the kingdom. Even good laws do not have that kind of effect.

And if the law couldn't enable you to live a righteous life *before* you knew Christ, neither can it do that afterwards. Christians can easily see their life as a list of do's and don't's. They can then become consumed by guilt when they fail to live up their list. It transpires that they are living by the law.

All that law can do for us is make us aware that we are sinners – and drive us to Christ.

Frame 2: Christ binned the law

Then came the moment when we were discharged from the law.

- If you **covenant** a payment to a charity and die before fulfilling it, the would-be beneficiary cannot claim the money. Death terminates the arrangement. That is true with our relationship with law (as it was with our relationship with sin, see chapter 6). Christ died to the law; and because he died as our representative, in effect we have died to the law. Christ rose to a new life; so do we.
- **Marriage** too is terminated by death, so a person is then free to remarry. Our death means the end of our marriage to the law, and the beginning of a new marriage to Christ. After that death we come to belong to someone else, so that we can bear fruit to God.

Frame 3: A new partnership

Being married has its obligations. Before, you could do what you liked, when you liked; now you have to take someone else into account. There are responsibilities, pressures and expectations that you hadn't really thought about. The new life will only really work if you recognize that and live by it.

So it is with the end of our old marriage to the law and the beginning of our new marriage to Christ. It is the end of servitude, but not the end of service. It's moving from a legal, institutional relationship to right and wrong, to an organic personal one:

- Under the **old** relationship, God makes the rules and watches out for people disobeying them.
- Under the **new** relationship, God leaves us free to do the things that God wants, without there being rules to attempt to *make* us do so.

So the works of the flesh are replaced by the fruit of the Spirit (Galatians 5:19-23). Paul is promising (rather than requiring) that these fruits will grow in your life.

TWO-STAGE CHRISTIANITY?

The last section of Romans 7 speaks of a struggle to do what is right.

Is this the struggle of someone who is living the Christian life on a lower level, who hasn't yet found the complete release that Christ can bring, who hasn't yet been completely taken over by the Spirit? Is the Christian life essentially a two-stage affair – first and second blessing, conversion then baptism in the Spirit? If so, the lower-level Christian is the one who is still living in Romans 7 and hasn't moved on to Romans 8. Christian leaders like Martyn Lloyd Jones have taught this.

There are several weaknesses to this kind of theory:

- It ignores the fact that every spiritual blessing is given us in Christ when we respond to him.
- It produces two categories of Christians, whereas Paul assumes there is only one.
- Paul talks about his experience of struggle as if it's going on now – which is at least careless if he is referring to something essentially past.

There are two other theories. Paul may be speaking of his present experience as a mature Christian, that he was constantly involved in an agonising conflict between flesh and Spirit. This is how Calvin interpreted it. But would Paul really describe himself as 'carnal'?

Or Paul may be describing an *un*believer, so that the deliverance he speaks of is the deliverance that comes from trusting in Christ. The scholar Ernst Käsemann takes this line. But unbelievers don't usually feel torn apart by the conflict that is described here, and it is difficult on this view to make sense of the last verse of the chapter.

But the main point of this passage isn't to relate anyone's personal experience. It's to reassert Paul's concern that obeying rules can never make you holy. That's true whether you are an unbeliever, or a person under conviction of sin, or a not-very-advanced Christian, or a mature person in Christ. Christ has rescued us from a life of obedience to rules, so that we may belong to him and bear fruit for God.

HEIRS TO EVERYTHING

Read Romans 8:1-39 as you study these pages. Make notes on particular things you learn; use the box on page 36.

The vantage-point for understanding Romans 8 as a whole is verse 17:

- We are God's children.
- Therefore we share Christ's position as God's heir.
- Therefore we will share Christ's glory.
- Therefore we must share Christ's suffering.

Being God's children

Broadly, there are two ways we have experienced our parents relating to us. We have seen how our memory of childhood (and our experience of adulthood) can be one in which our parents seem to dominate us and make us feel guilty (see page 25). I am grateful to God and to my parents that my own experience was very different. My father was an ordinary working man who knew nothing about theology. My life and work were as much of a mystery to him as his were to me. But I know he loved me and would give me his last penny if he felt I needed it.

Paul describes these two kinds of experience as:

- **the spirit of a slave** which makes us fall back into fear
- **the spirit of a son or daughter** which enables us to call out 'Abba, Father.'

The Spirit bears witness to our spirit that we are children of God – and if we are God's children, then we are God's heirs. We share Christ's position in relation to his Father. He looked into his Father's face with the same confidence as I looked into my father's, and as I hope my sons can look into mine. We share Christ's relationship to his Father, however ambivalent we may feel about our earthly fathers.

We can cry 'Abba, Father' as Jesus did. But only once are we told that Jesus did that – in Gethsemane (Mark 14:36). That 'Abba, Father' expressed not only confidence in relating to God, but also commitment. In saying it, Jesus submitted to the will of the one in whom he had confidence.

For us too, 'Abba, Father' is the cry of joyful trust and security, but also the cry of solemn commitment and submission. To be led by the Spirit of God has nothing to do with 'feeling led' to pray in a certain way or suggest a certain hymn. The Spirit's leading is the Spirit driving us into a way of life which is the opposite of the way the flesh leads (see v. 9, 12).

Sharing Christ's suffering

When a princess becomes a queen, she is transformed from being a relatively ordinary person, able to go out shopping like everyone else, to being enthroned, crowned and bowed down to. She becomes a different person. We too will be transformed. We were not born into a royal family, but we have been adopted into one and have become Christ's brothers and sisters. We therefore will share his glory.

But our experience now may seem distinctly non-glorious, not merely ordinary but characterized by weakness and affliction. We groan, and ask who will deliver us from this.

The question of suffering is the most demanding one we ever face, as we seek to make sense of our losses and pains. Paul gives us six things to remember as we wrestle with it:

- **Suffering is the only way to glory** (v. 17). Trouble is not a strange experience which makes you wonder whether you are on the way to glory. It is the only road to glory, as Jesus' story shows (and his is the glory that we share). It is not that we will be glorified *despite* suffering, or if suffering doesn't get us first, but that we suffer *and* are glorified with him.

- **The suffering does not compare with the glory** (v. 18). A woman's pain in childbirth is forgotten when she has her baby at the breast (see v. 22-23).

- **The Spirit's presence helps us experience the glory** even in the midst of the suffering (v. 23). The Spirit belongs to the age to come, the age of glory. If you are talking about living the life of the new world, the Spirit is the way to do that. If you are speaking of having a little experience of glory now which keeps us going in the context of adversity, it is the Spirit who makes that possible. The Spirit brings the presence of final glory into today.

- **The Spirit intercedes for us in our suffering** on the way to glory (v. 26). When we do not how to pray, the Spirit knows how to pray for us.

- **Everything works together for good for those who love God** (v. 28), and our suffering is part of that. So when something happens which seems incompatible with God's purpose or God's love, we are invited to write over it, 'This is part of the everything', part of what God uses to take us from justification to glory (v. 29-30).

- **The suffering isn't worth comparing with the love** of Christ which we know now, never mind about the glory of the future (v. 31-39).

GROWING INTO IT?

The process of walking in the Spirit's way is often spoken of as the way of sanctification, of gradually growing more holy. Yet in Romans 5-8 there is no specific reference to growing - the nearest to it comes in Romans 5:3-4, and even there it is only implicit. Indeed in the New Testament as a whole, references to growing as a Christian are quite rare. It is not the central model for understanding the dynamics of the Christian life.

In our culture we understand everything in terms of growth and development, whether it is biology, economics, theology or a relationship with God. The Bible thinks in terms of discontinuities and breaks, more than of unfolding developments:

- this age and the age to come
- flesh and spirit
- what we once were and what we now are in Christ
- law and grace
- bondage and freedom
- death and life
- wrath and peace

It does not say 'You are on the way from this age to the age to come', partly flesh partly spirit, growing out of bondage into freedom. It assumes that we are one thing or the other, and that it is up to us to decide what we are.

We don't have to say, 'Well, maybe next year I will be able to face that challenge.' All the resources of God's grace through Christ are available to us in the Holy Spirit now. And if we refuse them, we are in the flesh, in bondage, under law, dead in trespasses and sins.

We are under obligation to follow the leading of the Spirit of God, as people who share Christ's relationship to his Father.

God's part and ours

How does all that come about? It involves:

- God acting for us, in Christ
- God speaking to us to tell us about it, in the Bible
- God working within us, by the Spirit

It also involves us. It is we who cry, 'Abba, Father', who walk in the Spirit's way, who pay attention to the Spirit's priorities rather than the flesh's, who put to death the deeds of the body. We do not have to. We can carry on living the flesh's way. Or we can look at what God has done, listen to what He says, cry 'Abba, Father', and walk in the Spirit's ways. That is what happens when we share Christ's relationship to his Father.

MARTYN LLOYD-JONES

(1899-1983)

David Martyn Lloyd-Jones was a doctor who gave up medicine to become a pastor. For four decades he was minister of Westminster Chapel in London, where week by week he preached his way through biblical book after biblical book. Famous jokes relate how missionaries come back to Britain after years of service overseas – to find he is only three verses further on than when they left. He is *the* 20th century Puritan-style expositor. The following excerpt comes from *Spiritual Depression* (a book of 21 sermons on Psalms 42-43...).

Let me sum it up in this way, therefore. You and I – and to me this is one of the great discoveries of the Christian life; I shall never forget the release which realizing this for the first time brought to me – you and I must never look at our past lives; we must never look at any sin in our past life in any way except that which leads us to praise God and to magnify His grace in Christ Jesus. I challenge you to do that. If you look at your past and are depressed by it, if as a result you are feeling miserable as a Christian, you must do what Paul did. 'I was a blasphemer,' he said, but he did not stop at that. Does he then say: 'I am unworthy to be a preacher of the gospel'? In fact he says the exact opposite: 'I thank Christ Jesus our Lord who hath enabled me, for that He counted me faithful putting me into the ministry, etc.'. When Paul looks at the past and sees his sin he does not stay in a corner and say: 'I am not fit to be a Christian, I have done such terrible things'. Not at all. What it does to him, its effect upon him, is to make him praise God. He glories in grace and says: 'And the grace of our Lord was exceeding abundant with faith and love which is in Christ Jesus'.

That is the way to look at your past. So, if you look at your past and are depressed, it means that you are listening to the devil. But if you look at the past and say: 'Unfortunately it is true I was blinded by the god of this world, but thank God His grace was more abundant, He was more than sufficient and His love and mercy came upon me in such a way that it is all forgiven, I am a new man', then all is well. That is the way to look at the past, and if we do not do that, I am almost tempted to say that we deserve to be miserable. Why believe the devil instead of believing God? Rise up and realize the truth about yourself, that all the past has gone, and you are one with Christ, and all your sins have been blotted out once and for ever. O let us remember that it is sin to doubt God's word, it is sin to allow the past, which God has dealt with, to rob us of our joy and our usefulness in the present and in the future. Hear again those words uttered from heaven to the doubtful, hesitant Apostle Peter: 'What God hath cleansed, that call not thou common'. Rejoice in this wondrous grace and mercy that has blotted out your sins and made you a child of God. 'Rejoice in the Lord always, and again I say rejoice.'

WATCHMAN NEE

(1903-1972)

Watchman Nee (Ni To-sheng) was a leader of the independent churches in China. His teaching was put into written form, and these books became spiritual classics in the 1950s and 1960s. They include *The Normal Christian Life*, *Release of the Spirit*, and *What Shall This Man Do?*. The following comes from *Sit, Walk, Stand*, based on Ephesians.

'God... made him to sit... and made us to sit with him.' Let us first consider the implications of this word 'sit'. As we have said, it reveals the secret of a heavenly life. Christian life does not begin with walking; it begins with sitting. The Christian era began with Christ, of whom we are told that, when He had made purification of sins, He 'sat down on the right hand of the Majesty on high' (Heb 1:3). With equal truth we can say that the individual Christian life begins with a man 'in Christ' – that is to say, when by faith we see ourselves seated together with Him in the heavens.

Most Christians make the mistake of trying to walk in order to be able to sit, but that is a reversal of the true order.

'Sitting' is an attitude of rest. Something has been finished, work stops, and we sit. It is paradoxical, but true, that we only advance in the Christian life as we learn first of all to sit down.

What does it really mean to sit down? When we walk or stand we bear on our legs all the weight of our own body, but when we sit down our entire weight, no matter how heavy we are, rests upon the chair or couch on which we sit. We grow weary when we walk or stand, but we feel rested when we have sat down for a while. In walking or standing we expend a great deal of energy, but when we are seated we relax at once, because the strain no longer falls upon our muscles and nerves but upon something outside of ourselves. So also in the spiritual realm, to sit down is simply to rest our whole weight – our load, ourselves, our future, everything – upon the Lord. We let Him bear the responsibility and cease to carry it ourselves.

But if what we have said is true of the forgiveness of our sins and of the gifts of the Holy Spirit, what about our sanctification? ... Again the secret is not in walking but in sitting; not in doing anything but in resting in something done. 'We *died* to sin.' We '*were baptised*... into his death.' 'We *were buried* with him.' 'God... *quickened* us together with Christ.' (Rom 6:2,3,4, Eph 2:5) All these statements are in the past (aorist) tense. Why is this? Because the Lord Jesus was crucified outside Jerusalem nearly two thousand years ago, and *I was crucified with him.* This is the great historic fact. By it His experience has now become my spiritual history, and God can speak of me as already having everything 'with Him'. All that I now have I have 'with Christ'.

JIM PACKER

(1931-)

James I. Packer taught in English theological colleges for many years and has always been cast for the role of the great modern Evangelical systematic theologian. He has never taken up this role – apparently because he is more interested in the link between theology and spirituality. His best-known book in this connection is *Knowing God*, but I have more appreciated *A Quest For Godliness: The Puritan Vision of the Christian Life* from which these two quotations come. They also introduce you to Puritan writing on spirituality.

Spiritual authority is hard to pin down in words, but we recognise it when we meet it. It is a product compounded of conscientious faithfulness to the Bible; vivid perception of God's reality and greatness; inflexible desire to honour and please him; deep self-searching and radical self-denial; adoring intimacy with Christ; generous compassion manward; and forthright simplicity, God-taught and God-wrought, adult in its knowingness while childlike in its directness. The man of God has authority as he bows to divine authority, and the pattern of God's power in him is the baptismal pattern of being supernaturally raised from under burdens that feel like death.

* * * * *

When this supernatural assurance dawns, it transforms a man's entire Christian life. 'It is a new conversion,' says Goodwin; 'it will make a man differ from himself in what he was before in that manner almost as conversion doth before he was converted. There is a new edition of all a man's graces.' This sounds startling, but Goodwin means what he says, and works the idea out. Assurance, he tells us, increases faith (faith 'receives a new degree'); and this invigoration of faith results in a new release of energy at every point in one's Christian life.

In the first place, it deepens one's communion with the Triune God in meditating on the 'plot' of redeeming love.

In assurance... a man's communion and converse is... sometimes with the Father, then with the Son, and then with the Holy Ghost; sometimes his heart is drawn out to consider the Father's love in choosing, and then the love of Christ in redeeming, and so the love of the Holy Ghost, that searcheth the deep things of God, and revealeth them to us, and taketh all the pains with us...

Nor is this all. The coming of assurance quickens the spiritual understanding: by it 'the eye of the soul is strengthened to see further into truths; all truths are more clearly known by this'. It makes a man bold and powerful in prayer. It makes him holier, though he was holy before: 'all assurance that is true assurance... maketh a man holy'; 'nothing makes the heart more in the love, study, practice, and growth of holiness, than the glorious testimony of the Holy Spirit.' Assurance makes a man tireless in Christian service: 'when once... the love of God is shed abroad in a man's heart, it makes a man work for God ten times more than before'; 'assurance will strongly put men upon the winning of others... A soul under assurance is unwilling to go to heaven without company.' Finally, assurance brings with it the 'joy unspeakable and full of glory' of 1 Peter 1:8, which is one of Goodwin's favourite texts in this connection. Such assurance as this, so far from encouraging presumption and laziness, is in fact the strongest possible incentive against sin, for its possessor knows that by sinning he will jeopardise his assurance, prompting God to withdraw it, and there is nothing that he is more anxious to avoid than that. These, then, are the chief fruits of assurance.

YOUR NOTES

On Romans 5

On Romans 6

On Romans 7

On Romans 8

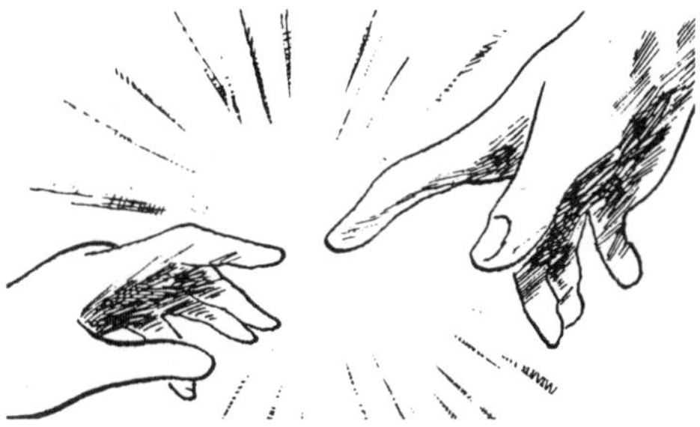

Unit 4

THE 'SPIRIT' IN SPIRITUALITY

PURPOSE

This Unit deals with the Holy Spirit, including the 'gifts' the Spirit brings to the Church.

People differ enormously in their experience of the 'blessing' or 'baptism' in the Holy Spirit and in their attitude to such things. Whatever your own previous experience, here is an opportunity to think through the issues – and to put your conclusions into practice in your own spiritual life.

CONTENTS

The material on these pages, and on pages 52-53, is by Adrian Chatfield.

THE SPIRIT THROUGH THE AGES

In our age, influenced as it has been by the renewal movement, it has sometimes been tempting to think that people had not really experienced the Holy Spirit acting in the Church before. Actually the Spirit has been bringing about different forms of renewal over the centuries.

The call of the desert

In the Christianity of 3rd century Egypt, the church had become complacent. Some began to hunger for a church that would take God so seriously that nothing else would matter. St **Antony** and others started developing a monastic ideal which was willing to give up everything for God.

One of the roots of Pentecostalism lies in not letting anyone be more important to you than God. It is a reaction against the suggestion that it is fine to be a Christian as long as you are not too extreme.

The return to simplicity

Over the centuries monasticism waxed and waned. People can become comfortable even in a monastery, and the monastic rules, intended to regulate a life of simplicity, became complicated. There then developed a desire to return to 'apostolic simplicity' and a Bible-based model of the church. St **Francis** and St **Clare** wanted to strip off unnecessary accretions to the contemporary understanding of discipleship. **Francis** in particular was prepared to risk looking stupid for the sake of keeping the Christian life simple. If you only have room for a few things, you need to know what those few things are.

The recovery of the Word

In the 14th century John **Wycliffe**'s concern was the recovery of the Word of God for the people of God, while the **Lollards** engaged in the contemporary equivalent of Bible smuggling. Their conviction was that 'priestcraft' needed to be eliminated so that the people could have the Bible for themselves.

Here are the roots of the belief that the Bible was designed to be read and understood by ordinary people. It was a new thought then.

The reformation of the church

In the 16th century the radical reformation, beginning with the **Anabaptists** in the 1520s, was equivalent to the House Church movement of our day. It saw itself as building the true temple or the true church – not constructing it anew on the site of the old church's ruins, but starting again. It had a vision of the church as the pure bride of Christ, and wanted to see that vision become reality.

The small group movement

Methodism was founded on a movement that began in London in 1699, a movement of small groups gathering to deepen people's faith. It

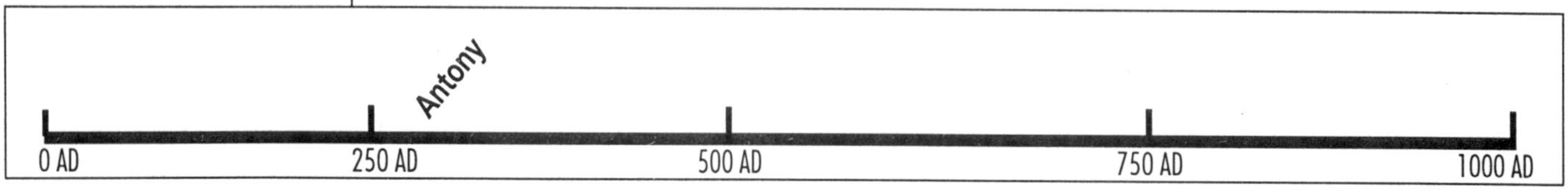

presupposed that it was not enough to gather on Sundays as the whole people of God. People needed something that involved more personal commitment and worked more methodically. In due course this became the Methodist system of 'classes'. It believed that it was not enough to know that you were justified: you had to live a holy life.

Methodism's concern for holiness (or 'sanctification') eventually led to the development of **Pentecostalism** with its stress on the involvement of the Holy Spirit in sanctification. The Methodist movement also signified a movement from the church building out into the highways and byways, as George **Whitfield** convinced the **Wesleys** that they had to go out to preach. Thus both Methodism and Pentecostalism signified a de-churchifying of Christianity and a radicalizing of everything.

The holiness movement

The distinctive feature of the holiness movement was a challenge to receive a 'second blessing' after conversion. It believed that people needed to be born again *and* to be baptized in the Spirit if the tendency to besetting sin was to be stripped away. It was this overwhelming experience of the power of God which drove Charles **Finney** into his evangelistic ministry.

The charismatic movement

Pentecostalism is often said to have been born in 1900, but similar phenomena are reported from the Scottish church in 1829 and from India in the 1850s. It is not something which can be dated. It was born out of God doing things that the church would not allow. The freedom of the Spirit was reasserted.

But this always tended to lead to a reassertion of control by the people who had found the freedom. In Pentecostalism and in the charismatic movement the rules were broken – but then leaders emerged who sought to calm things down and to confine power and authority to themselves.

African spirituality

Modern African renewal at the beginning of the 20th century was a movement from the USA to Africa. But the movement between the two continents had earlier been the other way. The significance of African spirituality lies in its influence on Euro-American spirituality as Africans moved to America. This changed American Christianity, giving it conviction about the power of God. It opened the American church up to the ministry of healing, visions, ecstatic experience, and an awareness of evil spirits and the need to cast them out. This movement believed that experience of God's fullness can be repeated – Caribbean Christianity assumes that the experience of baptism in the Spirit can be repeated many times.

The marginalized

The influence of African spirituality illustrates how important the marginalized have been to the renewal of the church. The marginalized are the people who aren't in power, don't have influence and don't count, because of their race, their class or their gender.

Characteristically, the people who were originally marginal are re-marginalized as the movement develops. The place of black people within Pentecostalism is an example. So also is the significance of women to the history of these renewal movements. Women were prominent in the leadership of early Methodism, but men took over and put the women back in their place.

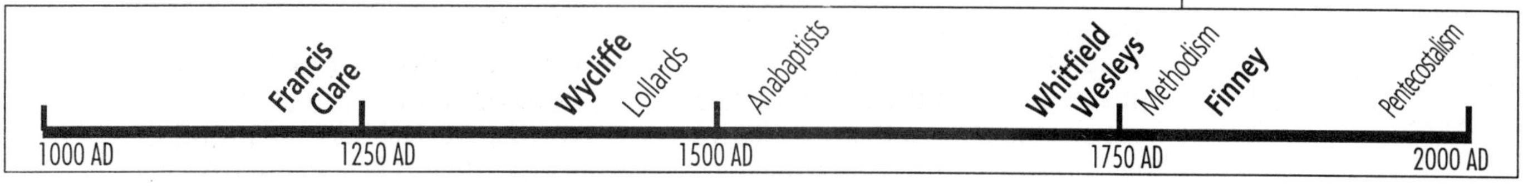

BAPTISM IN THE HOLY SPIRIT

The phrase 'baptism in the Spirit' has recently been important in the charismatic movement to describe an experience of God separate from conversion – an experience which brought new fullness of spiritual life, often to people who had been Christians for years. This understanding of the phrase goes back to the Holiness movement of the 19th century, as one way of describing the 'second blessing' which could follow on conversion. It then became a key term in Pentecostalism as *the* way of describing that experience – although the phrase was not confined to the 'second blessing', and sometimes referred to a *third* experience of God's Spirit, after both conversion and sanctification.

John the Baptist spoke of the future baptism of Jesus as one in which you would be 'baptized with the Holy Spirit and with fire' (Matthew 3:11). In a sense Jesus did this at Pentecost, when the disciples were filled with the Spirit and something like fire appeared among them. But he has kept on doing something similar for the Christian community ever since.

Baptized with the Spirit

God makes promises in the Old Testament regarding an overwhelming outpouring of His Spirit. From these we can see that being overwhelmed in the Holy Spirit will mean:

- **we will say** things we haven't said before, see things we haven't seen before (Joel 2:28-29).
- **we will think** things we haven't thought before, do things we haven't done before: our stone-hard, inflexible minds will become fleshly and flexible (Ezekiel 36:26).
- **we will hope** things when we would otherwise have given up hope, and experience new life (Ezekiel 37:1-11) .
- **we will see** God act again (Isaiah 63:7-14).
- **our leaders** will become leaders who work with wisdom and knowledge and the fear of the Lord, for fairness and peace (Isaiah 11:1-5).
- **our commitment** to God will become reality instead of just words; we will become proud to speak of God (Isaiah 44:1-5).

SIGNS OF BAPTISM

We may expect that there will be 'signs' of being baptized in the Spirit or filled with the Spirit, and these may include speaking in tongues or falling over. But in the long term the question is rather whether the signs are those which appear in the Old Testament promises listed on this page.

Baptized with fire

Matthew (3:11) and Luke (3:16) both have John speaking of 'baptism in Spirit and fire', which sounds both encouraging and threatening. But Mark (1:8) and John (1:33) have him speaking only of 'baptism in Spirit'. The same is true of Acts (1:5, 11:16) and of 1 Corinthians (12:13), the only other places where the phrase appears. One effect is to make this baptism sound less threatening – which fits the way this experience is spoken of in the church today.

But in the context of Scripture, even talk of 'baptism in Spirit' (without reference to fire) would be threatening. In Luke 12:49-50 fire and baptism both suggest disaster. In Isaiah 4:4 cleansing comes through the purging effect of the spirit, in judgment and burning.

Luke 12:49-50 suggests that Jesus takes that judgment element in baptism into himself. He does not *administer* the sign of judgment – he *receives* it. This fits with the way subsequent parts of the New Testament talk. Because Jesus has undergone his baptism of fire, we do not have to. We simply enjoy baptism in the Holy Spirit.

How many baptisms?

When John proclaimed his baptism, it seems to have been a once-for-all rite of preparation for the imminent coming of God's rule in Israel, although in Israel there were lots of water-ceremonies which conveyed ongoing cleansing. Baptism in water is similarly a once-for-all rite: you can only be baptized into Christ once, as you can only marry someone once.

- 1 Corinthians 12:13 implies that baptism in the Spirit is part of what goes on when you come to know Christ, and so any experience which comes to us later is not baptism in the Spirit. Yet what happens in Acts 11:16 shows that in practice God is sometimes willing to work in untidy ways.

- 1 Corinthians 12:13 also talks of our drinking of the Spirit. That is another way of describing what happens when we come to faith in Christ. But Ephesians 5:16 urges us to be filled with the Spirit on an ongoing basis: this is not merely a once-for-all experience.

In the church over the centuries, many people have wanted to go through their baptism more than once. But perhaps this is more like couples who want to renew their marriage vows. I know a couple who were married in a registry office before they were Christians, and who have often hankered after a 'proper' wedding, a way of making their promises before God. It would be quite reasonable for them to have a ceremony which wasn't quite a wedding, but was an opportunity for them to consciously make their promises before God for the first time. Another way of seeing the tumultuous experience of being overwhelmed by the Holy Spirit some time after conversion, is to see it as a delayed honeymoon.

WHO NEEDS IT?

In Isaiah, who needed to be overwhelmed by a baptism of fire?

The Acquisitive: People who were only interested in accumulating property and land, till there was no room for anyone else in the land. They were not interested in people, in the community, in relationships. They shut the door on other people. (Isaiah 5:8)

The Audience: People who were only interested in entertainment, in parties, in indulging themselves. 'Bring a bottle' was their favourite exhortation. This diverted them from seeing what God was doing. (Isaiah 5:11-12)

The Apathetic: People who had stopped believing in the passionate God of Isaiah, the God of love and energy, the God who raged and cared. They had lost the passion of their faith in that God and got cynical. (Isaiah 5:19)

The Avoiders: People who weren't prepared to acknowledge the difference between joy and hurt, between calamity and blessing. They would deny suffering, deny the cross. (Isaiah 5:20)

The Addicted: People who were overly enthusiastic about worship and experience and anything impressive. (Isaiah 1:11-15)

In other words, they were very modern worshippers...

FIRE AND SPIRIT

Talk of the Spirit can itself be threatening as well as encouraging. And conversely fire can be encouraging as well as threatening – as it is in Acts 2. Fire purges – its burning is creative (see Isaiah 1:25, 6:6-7).

STILL FREE?

In the New Testament, there are no hints of how to seek for the baptism in the Spirit for ourselves or for someone else. It is something that 'happens' rather than something that you try to make happen. All people do is pray or tell other people the story of Jesus. Since then, people have often tried to tell us how to seek this baptism. Perhaps this is a way of asserting 'control' over God's activity rather than allowing God to be free?

GIFTS OF GRACE

Grace and gift

'Grace' is one of the most important terms in theology. In everyday life it means the unearned and undeserved favour that one person will sometimes show to another person in need. It is thus used to refer to the undeserved favour that God shows to humanity in giving Christ to die for the world. God's grace finds further concrete expression in the life of God's people in producing the fruit of the Spirit.

That same grace also grants the 'gifts' of the Spirit spoken of in the New Testament. The usual word for 'grace' is *charis*; the usual word for spiritual gift is *charisma*. So ministries such as those of apostles, prophets, teachers, miracle-workers, healers, helpers, administrators, and speakers in various kinds of tongues (1 Corinthians 12:28) are 'grace-things', graces made concrete.

The Spirit in action

The background of 'spirit', like that of 'grace', lies in human experience. A person's *spirit* is the vital life in them (the word also means *breath*). It is their energy, drive and power, showing itself in decisiveness, activity, excitement and courage, and pushing them into action. So God's spirit encapsulates God's dynamic and drive at work in the world.

The Old Testament speaks of God's *creative* work as an activity of God's spirit. God's spirit (or God's *wind*) moved over the Deep and ordered the heavens. At the creation of each individual person or animal, it is God's spirit (*breath*) that gives them life by giving them breath; it is also God who ends life by withdrawing this spirit/breath. So any person or animal who is alive has God's 'spirit' in them. At the re-creation of the world, the pouring out of God's spirit will transform devastation into fruitfulness, justice and peace.

Jesus in his ministry brings that renewal which the Old Testament associated with the *final* work of God's spirit. After his death and resurrection, his disciples live on in this age, looking for the time when they will be fully yielded to God's spirit. And they experience God's spirit present among them, the spirit who gives a foretaste of that final transformation now.

REFERENCES

For this paragraph, see Genesis 1:2; 6:3; Job 26:13; 27:3; 32:8; 33:4; 34:14; Psalm 104:29-30; Ecclesiastes 12:7; Isaiah 32:14-20; 42:5.

For the next paragraph, see Mark 1:7-12; Luke 4:14-21; Acts 2; Romans 8; 2 Corinthians 4:7-5:10; Ephesians 1:3-22.

THE MIXED BLESSING?

The churches of the New Testament varied in their experience of these spiritual graces-in-action. Some knew them well, some had got into a mess with them, and some (to judge from the Epistles) may not have been acquainted with them at all.

Old Testament Israel too saw some things as the direct activity of the spirit of God; but as in the New Testament, the way people experienced this varied.

Such variety of experience in Israel's life and in the life of the early church parallels the variety of experience and attitudes in the contemporary church.

- One church may be experiencing Corinthian excitement at the presence and activity of the Holy Spirit, believing that God is at work in its midst by means of prophecy and healing.
- Another may be quite unaware that such things are going on in the church today.
- A third may be lurching through a cycle of re-discovery, high expectation and sad disappointment, as they hope for a breakthrough into ultimate spiritual blessing through some key grace (tongues, then prophecy, then healing, then exorcism, then being slain in the Spirit ...).
- Another church may have assimilated such graces into its normal life in a fairly painless way.
- Yet another may feel a wistful (or superior) puzzlement at the exotic happenings it hears of elsewhere.

Gifts with character

Overleaf we will look at the characteristics of each of these graces, these expressions of grace. But what characterises them (or should do so) as a whole?

❶ Diversity with a purpose

Their diversity is like the parts of a body. They are given to benefit the congregation as a whole, and to upbuild it by working together. If people come to overvalue particular graces, this 'working as a whole' is compromised. If people are led into a false individual assurance about what God has told them, and despise or ignore the graces given to others, the corporate nature of Christian insight and guidance is lost.

❷ Emotional and rational

The graces which involve speaking combine an emotional component with a rational one.

- Some Christians are drawn to an **emotional**, non-rational faith which instinctively rejoices in tongues, 'singing in the Spirit' and singing Scripture verses out of context. Paul's message to them is that God gave them their minds as well as their emotions, and that even in their praise and prayer their mind as well as their spirit should be fruitful (1 Corinthians 14:13-15).

- Other Christians are drawn to an **intellectual**, rational faith which instinctively rejoices in a more reflective, cerebral spirituality. Paul invites them to be more free with their emotions, glad that even he, the profound theologian, speaks in tongues more than all the Corinthians do – no mean claim! (1 Corinthians 14:18).

❸ An enhanced humanity

In the operation of all these graces, God takes the natural and makes it supernatural. They are not grafted onto the natural – they are potential or actual human abilities which are liberated, directed or refined by being brought into the service of God. The fullness of the Spirit frees people to be their true natural selves, and they are then able to manifest gifts that might otherwise never have found expression and do things that they might otherwise have been unable to do. So the graces involve a full realization of human potential *and* an openness to God's intervening in human life.

❹ Relevant to context

Graces are specific to contexts. They serve the needs of the church to which they are given. Some of the New Testament graces are so specific to their context that we are uncertain today exactly what they originally entailed. Accepting the New Testament as our authority does not necessarily imply expecting all these graces to be in evidence in Spirit-filled church life today. Nor can we exclude the possibility of other graces unmentioned in the New Testament being given by God to meet the specific needs of *our* context, such as counselling or spiritual direction. Music and other art forms are contemporary graces in the church, linking as much with Old Testament antecedents (crafts, architecture) as with New Testament ones. And the Old Testament might suggest other avenues of gifting – like liberation and political prophecy.

❺ Acting with attitude

The graces-in-action are designed to give 'body' to the graces-of-attitude, the harvest of the Spirit (Galatians 5:22-23) – and they are ideally designed to do so. Caring, joy, peace, tolerance, kindness, generosity, trustworthiness, humility, self-discipline – all find natural expression in graces-in-action such as prophecy, acts of compassion, teaching, healing, tongues and giving.

Yet like the rest of God's good creation, they can equally be harnessed to the old nature with its sexual immorality, alien worship, personal enmity, jealousy, divisiveness and self-indulgence (Galatians 5:19-21). These attitudes and practices are the antithesis of being led by the Spirit, but they have sometimes characterised those who have exercised 'spiritual gifts'.

GRACES OF WORD

An essential feature of the graces of the Spirit is their diversity. 1 Peter 4:10 talks about God's grace 'in varied forms', a phrase which originally meant 'multi-coloured'. 'Multi-coloured grace' would be an overtranslation, but it is suggestive.

Elsewhere the point is made by listing the graces in their variety:

- **Romans 12:6-7** – prophecy, service, teaching, encouragement, giving, leadership, showing compassion.
- **1 Corinthians 12:8-10, 28** – wisdom, knowledge, faith, healing, miracles, prophecy, discernment, tongues, interpretation of tongues.
- **Ephesians 4:11** - apostles, prophets, evangelists, pastors, teachers.

1 Peter 4:11 implies two main categories, those involving **speaking** and those involving **serving**. We look first at the 'speaking' graces.

Apostleship

Apostleship comes first in two of the lists. Apostles were the envoys Christ specifically commissions to spread the message about him.

The term is often applied (especially in Luke-Acts) to the original twelve disciples, but elsewhere in the New Testament it can refer to other pioneer missionary evangelists through whom Christian communities were founded. This meaning makes sense in the lists of graces, as all the graces are expected to appear in each individual church' but it raises the question of the relationship of apostleship to the gift of an **evangelist**. Perhaps an evangelist was a more settled, church-based figure (see Acts 21:8, and 2 Timothy 4:5 perhaps). An apostle was one with a special calling from God, a special commission by a church, and perhaps an especially powerful ministry (for this last, see 2 Corinthians 12:12). They may also have been those who took the gospel to whole new groups (as in the expression 'the apostle to the Gentiles' which is used of Paul).

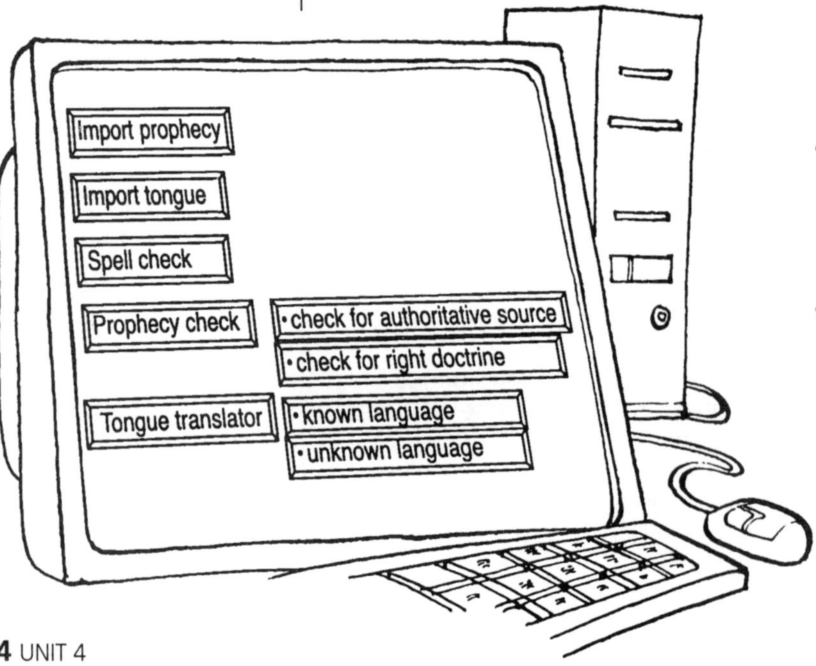

Prophecy

Prophecy follows apostleship in 1 Corinthians and Ephesians. It receives its most substantial discussion in 1 Corinthians 12-14, yet even such passages leave us in some uncertainty as to what Christian prophecy involved.

- If you begin from **Old Testament** prophecy in its classic form, you might expect Christian prophecy to be dominated by moral challenge and warning of judgment. John the Baptist comes nearest to this kind prophecy in the New Testament.
- If you begin from '**worship prophecy**' in the Old Testament, you would expect the bringing of (usually encouraging) words, especially to individuals – which has actually characterised recent charismatic renewal.
- If you begin from **1 Corinthians** 14, prophecy is a means of building up and encouraging a congregation gathered for worship.
- If you begin from **Revelation**, this spiritual challenge and encouragement is set in the context of promises of final judgment and salvation, and is expressed predominantly in Old Testament imagery and language (even though it does not directly quote Scripture).

- If you begin from specific prophecies in **Acts**, prophecy is the inspired prediction of future events with implications for the obligations or plans of particular communities or individuals (Acts 11:27-30, 21:10-14).

To make matters more complicated, it is difficult to see the relationship between prophecy and certain other graces, especially the utterance of **wisdom** and **knowledge**, **teaching**, and **encouragement**. Perhaps:

prophecy = passing on a message from God relating to the recipients' particular circumstances

teaching = instruction in the meaning and present implications of the faith, based on Scripture and needing no inspired status of its own

But it is impossible to be sure that this is the right distinction. Paul sees wisdom and knowledge embodied supremely in Christ, and perhaps 'utterances of wisdom' and 'knowledge' are words of teaching about Christ.

There is no biblical basis for understanding 'words of knowledge' as supernatural insight regarding a particular individual's needs – although there is sufficient biblical material for regarding such insight as a true gift. (See the story of Elisha.)

Tongues

Tongues is the grace which caused Paul most concern at Corinth. It apparently denotes words which are given to the speaker by God (thus far it resembles prophecy), but which the speaker does not understand. In Acts 2 on the first Christian Pentecost, these words are in other human languages which listeners could recognize. Elsewhere they are apparently in no human language – perhaps in the language of heaven (1 Corinthians 13:1)?

In Acts, one point about this strange form of speech is that it is an *evidence that God is at work in someone* (see Acts 10:44-48, 11:15-18). In this respect tongues parallels the ecstatic prophesy of Old Testament times (see 1 Samuel 10:6, 10) – though tongues is not ecstatic in the sense of beyond the person's control. Nor is tongues a *necessary* sign or consequence of being filled with the Holy Spirit.

The encouragement this grace brings makes it an edifying grace for the person who exercises it (1 Corinthians 14:4), though it is of little positive use to other believers or to unbelievers. If a person with this grace is to benefit others, they first need the further grace of being able to put God's message into words that other people can understand (I Corinthians 14:13).

If we are to guess the significance of tongues in itself for the person with the grace, then it may be that:

- the grace of tongues facilitates the expression of an **uninhibited opening of oneself to God**, of a worship which recognizes the inadequacy of human words to the praise of God. The significance of tongues would then approach that of mystical forms of prayer.
- the grace of tongues facilitates the expression of that **burdened petition and intercession** which cannot find words. If Romans 8:26-7 is referring to tongues, it is a New Testament reference to this kind of Christian prayer.

But much of this is inference from modern Christian experience rather than evidence from the New Testament itself.

Discernment

The grace of discernment becomes important once messages are brought by people with other 'speaking' graces. There is no guarantee at all that purported words from God are really from God, and it is the congregation's task, with the aid of those who have discernment, to weigh messages brought to it to see whether they recognize them as truly from God (1 Corinthians 12:9, 14:29, 1 John 4:1).

GRACES OF DEED

Some of the graces-in-action spoken of in the New Testament are expressed not in words but in deeds. But as with graces-of-word, the exact meaning of the terms used to describe individual graces is not always clear.

Acts of compassion

Acts of compassion is one of the more straightforward terms. Perhaps we can see it as made specific in the parable of judgment in Matthew 25:31-46. So it might involve:

- feeding the hungry
- giving drink to the thirsty
- inviting the stranger into one's house
- clothing the naked
- visiting the sick and imprisoned

Imagination and self-sacrifice seem likely to be integral to it.

Healing

Healing appears in both lists in 1 Corinthians 12. Its importance here and in other parts of the Bible lies in the conviction that God is concerned with people's well-being in all its aspects.

Human well-being belongs to that realm where the Spirit is active: primarily to that wholeness that is intrinsic to Beginning and End, but then to experiences of that activity in the present. Thus Jesus's own ministry brings healing to broken bodies, broken minds, broken spirits, and broken relationships, as a sign that he is the restorer of that wholeness; but total well-being continues to belong to the End. It is not experienced now.

This is true of all kinds of brokenness. Insofar as people experience new points of spiritual wholeness, then increasing physical wholeness may be expected to follow, because there is a oneness about the human person. As the church looks to realisations of the wholeness that belongs to the Beginning and the End, out-of-the-ordinary manifestations of that wholeness can be expected to appear.

So we should expect fruit from the exercise of the grace of healing. Yet total wholeness does belong to the End, and the reality of the healing ministry does not encourage over-simplified expectations of ministry to the sick, the mentally disturbed or the depressed. The theology of the cross, which Paul expounds to the Corinthians, includes his own experience of knowing God's power in the weakness of affliction. Paul had to cope with his 'thorn in the flesh', instead of being rescued from it as he prayed he would be. But in such experiences, wholeness is experienced in a paradoxical alternative form.

Exorcism

Loss of well-being also has its demonic aspect, and exorcism has a prominent place in contemporary charismatic ministry. It is a prominent feature of Jesus' own ministry and of the church in Acts, but it is noticeable that there is no clear reference to exorcism in the Epistles.

Deliverance from demonic power is part of the process of conversion for some people, and the Bible does seem to suggest that believers cannot come under the Devil's control – at least if they resist it.

Giving

Giving is a grace which receives extended treatment in 2 Corinthians 8-9, where Paul makes a point of playing on the link between the grace of Christ's self-giving and the grace of Christian self-giving to others. This expectation brings its challenge in different ways both to rich and to poor.

The grace of giving provides believers with a way of showing compassion to people who live far away, as well as people they can personally serve.

Other graces

Three other terms in Romans 12:8 and 1 Corinthians 12:28 are even more allusive. The NIV suggests they denote **leadership**, **helping others**, and **administration**. The middle of these is a technical term from banking – which might point to a rather down-to-earth grace of facilitating the kind of practical service that is the general concern of the graces-of-deed as a whole. The same might be true of administration. But with these too, one should expect something extraordinary by way of insight, imagination or self-sacrifice, if they are to count as 'spiritual gifts'.

Working of miracles and **faith** (presumably of a specially marked kind) (1 Corinthians 12:9, 10) may accompany or facilitate either graces-of-word or graces-of-deed, but they do not obviously belong under one or other heading. The same is true of several striking activities of the spirit of God in the Old Testament, such as the inspired leadership of Moses and Joshua, the inspired acts of liberation of the 'judges', and the inspired skills of the craftworkers of the tabernacle and the architect of the temple (Exodus 35; 1 Chronicles 28).

Before you go on to consider how you might enter more into these graces of God in your own life, as part of your life with God, pause to reflect on the questions that are raised for you. Divide them into two: intellectual questions about how to understand the graces, and personal questions about how you feel about them. Note them down below. This will help you 'clear the ground' for what follows.

Intellectual questions

✎

Personal questions

✎

ONE MAN'S JOURNEY

Spiritual gifts (or 'graces' as I have called them) are mainly for the upbuilding of the church – not for *my* benefit. But our concern here is their effect on our life with God and our relationship with Him. How does that work?

Here is something of my own experience, in the hope that it will help you with your own.

Tongues

I let myself babble in what I take to be tongues when I want to praise God in my private prayers but want to get away from words. Maybe words sometimes just require too much cerebral concentration. I do the same when I want to talk to God about some need of mine or of someone else, but I don't know what to ask.

Prophecies

During my time as Principal of St John's Nottingham, two prophecies were important to me.

- Before I became Principal a visiting minister (praying for the tutors) said, 'You had a vision for this college which you did not think would ever be fulfilled, but it will be fulfilled.'
- At my commissioning service, the preacher said, 'I will make the north wind your warmth, the snow your purity, the frost your brightness, and the night sky of winter your illumination.'

Both these were important resources and encouragements to me over the next ten years. They were also encouragements as I gave up being Principal and could see how God had made them come true.

Conversations with God

I quite often say things semi-aloud to God, and usually get responses.

- When I was going through a particularly tough period, I would simply cry out, 'Will it be all right?' and God always said 'Yes.'
- I quite often say 'I'm sorry I'm so stupid' – to which God usually replies 'You're not.'

Encouragement

I often need to talk to someone about the pressures of my job or about the pressures of looking after Ann. One encouragement is if people really do the classic thing of listening. It is *dis*couraging if they assume that they know what you are feeling, or if they cannot handle you telling them that things are hard.

Helping others

A friend of ours once gave us an electric kettle. We didn't know we needed an electric kettle until we had one. Ann had ceased to be able to use the gas cooker, and the electric kettle meant that she could now make herself a cup of coffee.

I doubt whether it is appropriate to call all helpfulness a matter of 'gift', but when someone does something especially imaginative and effective, Spirit and grace are involved.

Visions and pictures

For a year or two, a picture God gave me has been an important part of the framework of my life with God.

I am pushing Ann's wheelchair toward the horizon. I am viewing us from behind, so I see my back and a bit of the wheelchair – I can't actually see Ann. It's a bare landscape and quite a distance to the horizon towards which I push, but the ground is fairly level and the pushing just requires commitment and grit and persistence.

A key point is that it's a finite distance and that I can't see how far the journey goes beyond the horizon. In theory there may be many horizons to travel, but I don't have to visualize that long a journey – just the one horizon. Perhaps that may be the only one, and the pushing ends just beyond the visible horizon.

The other key point is that there's only the two of us, and thus only me pushing. A single horizon and a lone push – on my own by my willpower I can just manage one horizon at a time.

There are two alternative pictures which are nudging themselves upon me:

The longer view: My viewpoint changes, in the vertical plane – I zoom up, as happens in a film when the camera is elevated on a *simon snorkel* or a balloon. That means the horizon vastly lengthens, and I can see that the journey, the push, is much longer than I can see from ground level. There is no longer any avoiding of the prospect of the push lasting ten or twenty years, not just two or five. It may become more mountainous too.

An end to loneliness: Then the *simon snorkel* descends back to near ground level and I see other people, in ones and twos and threes, coming to join me behind the wheelchair. (I cry as I recall this bit.) Some are people I know, some are people I don't yet know, some are people I have known. Some just walk with me. Some take a handle. Some gently push me out of the way and push the wheelchair themselves. I notice that Ann is content as long as someone is pushing. I walk with them in the little crowd, content myself, more relaxed, unaccustomed to the luxury of walking without pushing. (I cry some more.) We talk quite a bit and laugh quite a bit. Someone ruffles my hair. The people change – some walk alongside for longer than others. The number of them changes – sometimes there are one or two, sometimes eight or ten. From where I am, because of the other people I can no longer see whether the countryside is bare, nor am I so aware of the distance to the horizons or of how far we travel.

DEVELOP YOUR GIFTS

How do you develop in the exercise of spiritual gifts? Speaking for myself, I have developed them by:

- **associating** with people who exercised gifts (e.g. being in a group which is trying to be 'open to God' together)
- **watching** for moments when God might be doing something along these lines with me – rather than assuming that this would never be the case
- **trying** things out (e.g. praying for someone's healing because they need it)
- **acknowledging** fears and then proceeding anyway – especially the fear that nothing will happen. (Other people might have different fears – like losing control.)
- **listening** to what other people say my gifts are (we are often very unreliable in our understanding of ourselves!)

HOW WHOLE CAN YOU GET?

MORE?

You might like to look at another book in the *Faith for Life* series, *In Search of Wholeness* by Russ Parker, Derek Fraser and David Rivers (St John's Extension Studies). This includes a Christian theology of healing and practical training in the healing ministry for church and medical settings.

This is not the place to discuss the ministry of healing as such. But in thinking about our life with God, our relationship with God, which also needs a measure of healing, we must be clear about the degree of healing to expect, and about how we open ourselves to greater wholeness.

The meaning of health

As human beings:

- we are body, mind, and spirit; all go to make up the person.
- we are not isolated individuals, but people in relationship with other persons.
- our relationships are not just one-to-one (e.g. with friends and family) but also one-to-community (e.g. with our village, church, ethnic group or factory).
- our personal relationships are not confined to human beings but also involve God.

Healing and health operate in relation to all of these – and they affect each other. Health and happiness involve positive well-being within my body, mind and spirit and in the interrelation between them; and it also involves a flourishing of my outward relationships with individuals, with communities and with God.

- Health in one area encourages health in another
- Sickness in one area encourages sickness in another
- Health in one area can offset sickness in another
- Sickness in one area can offset health in another

So a physically fit and well-off suburban British man may be less 'healthy' than an undernourished Ugandan woman – she may be living a happier life in which other parts of her life compensate for her physical undernourishment. The man may cease to live the life of someone who is justified by faith, over-work, and get 'flu (spiritual affects psychological and physical); then flu may make him depressed psychologically and spiritually (reverse movement).

It is also important to note that health at one stage of life is not health at another, in all these aspects and interrelations. A person is not like a machine, designed to function unchangingly throughout its life. A person is by nature a dynamic, developing, changing entity, on a journey from potential to maturity – and to death. Well-being at the age of 10, 30, 50 and 70 are different. God intends for you that state of physical, mental, social and spiritual well-being which is appropriate to each stage of your life.

What is 'health' for you at the moment? And where are the places of ill-health in your life with God (and in other areas of life, as it is all related)?

Getting healed

The Bible accepts the principle that you treat natural maladies by natural means: an angel gives a tired man a drink and a sandwich, and a sensible Samaritan knows how to apply bandages and primitive medicines (1 Kings 19:6-8; Luke 10:34).

It is admittedly a serious weakness of enterprises such as medicine, psychiatry and social work that they concern themselves with one aspect of the person in isolation from the others (not least people's relationship with God). But it is a serious weakness of some Christian approaches to healing that they fail to see these enterprises as God's means of bringing healing. We need to use them, but set them in a broader context.

God invites us to a holistic approach to healing, alongside a holistic approach to health.

- A prophet can combine fig poultice with exhortation (2 Kings 20:1-7)
- A king can be criticized for seeking help from doctors instead of from God (2 Chronicles 16:12. Was this recourse to medicine without asking the right spiritual questions?)

Complete health belongs to the End; any healing now is the Holy Spirit giving us anticipations of the End. If 'our spirits are alive' now through Christ, one can expect that even now 'God will give life to your mortal bodies' in some measure (Romans 8:10-11). If we are at peace with God, we should find peace in ourselves and with other people.

Not getting healed

We will not necessarily get healed.

There is no surprise about this. Because of what Christ has achieved, we can experience something of the well-being that belongs to the End. Heaven can begin to be reality now. But we cannot expect to experience *all* of it now – otherwise now would cease to be 'not the End'.

- 'We rejoice in God through our Lord Jesus Christ, through whom we have received the reconciliation.' (Romans 6:11)
- 'We groan inwardly as we wait for adoption as sons and daughters of God.' (Romans 8:23).

This tension is hard to maintain, and it is easier to resolve it:

- We can give up the expectation that God may do things now, and stop asking; then we risk the sad judgment of James 4:2, that we do not have because we do not ask.
- We can assume that healing is always possible, and that if it is not granted, there must be a special reason (usually the sin of the ill person or the lack of faith of the pray-ers).

There is no mystery about the fact that Christians experience cancer, depression, divorce, unemployment, road accidents, and eventually death itself. But even now the 'leaves of the tree of life are for the healing of the nations', and we are invited to reach out and pluck. We have to handle the fact that this may not be a moment when complete healing is available to us. And in exercising spiritual gifts in the service of others, we must become people who can help them to handle that fact too.

'We use medicine along with prayer to heal ourselves physically, [and we use] what is helpful in psychology along with prayer to heal us of fear, guilt, or hurt'

D. and M. Linn, *Healing of Memories*, Paulist Press, 1974, page 21

A NEW TESTAMENT MODEL

James 5:14-16 famously tells us what to do when we are ill. Presumably anointing with oil was in part a physical treatment (as in Luke 10:34), as well as having symbolic overtones. Oil helpfully embodied the interweaving of the spiritual and the physical. So James makes the assumption that physical illness raises questions about other aspects of the whole person's well-being.

In the process the focus may move away from the 'presenting problem' to some other issue, where the real need for healing lies. It may seem odd that the 'Signs and Wonders' approach to healing often involves words from God about sore elbows and the like – odd until you perceive that the sore elbow (and God's knowing and caring about it) is often the way into something else.

So James might suggest that what we do when we are ill is ask the congregation's elders to:

- look at us 'as a whole'
- listen to our confession
- assure us of God's forgiveness
- discern what is wrong with us, in the broader sense
- pray for our healing, in the narrower *and* the broader sense
- anoint us with oil
- see that we receive the appropriate treatment
- expect that we find healing, though perhaps on a different front from the one with which we started.

SPIRITUAL WARFARE

'Our struggle is not against flesh and blood, but... against the spiritual forces of evil in the heavenly realms.'
Ephesians 6:12

Jesus said to Peter, 'Get behind me, Satan.'
Matthew 16:23

The hard work involved in our life with God has a dimension to it which Christians today can easily fail to take account of. The Christian life is a struggle, but not just a struggle against our own lower self.

The Christian life involves resistance – not just against other people but against the one who can work through them. It is a battle which is going on whether or not we recognize or like it.

In British society today, people have stopped going to church but they have not stopped being religious. The crucial thing for people now is not belief but experience. The spread of charismatic evangelicalism can be seen as another example of this stress on experience. Spirituality thus becomes a search for life-enhancing and life-transforming experiences and for an internal spiritual balance. The god is ultimately the self.

If we want to prove that this is not true, we need to recognise that we are in a struggle and be committed to the discipline that will be necessary to win in the struggle.

'Consumer culture prioritizes experience – what's new and pleasurable – and this is applied to religion as well. The test is the quality of the experience, not the truth of the doctrine.'
Paul Heelas in the *Guardian*, 16 December 1996

Here are some key characteristics which lead to triumph in that struggle:

Renunciation

As people who sometimes do what is sinful, we are participants in a life that is 'of the devil' (1 John 3:8). So sin needs not merely repenting of but renouncing. When people are baptized they are asked whether they renounce the devil and all his works. In the early church this involved a public confession and renunciation. People destroyed idols, books and amulets. They helped to break down that other way of life which works against God.

Celebration

People who belong to Christ 'have overcome the evil one' (1 John 2:13). Why? Because the the devil has been defeated and thrown out of heaven, so he can no longer exercise any authority over us (Revelation 12:7-12). No 'principalities' (heavenly rulers) can separate us from God's love in Christ (Romans 8:38-39).

Celebration is part of spiritual warfare. It asserts this victory.

- Beating the bounds and 'Jesus marches' assert God's lordship over the area covered and claimed. They also push the boundaries further out.
- A positive side to the Anglican parish system is its declaration that all this territory belongs to God.
- In Anglo-Saxon times, rulers would place monasteries on the boundaries of their lands where the barbarians were (hence European monasteries are often in wild places) so that the prayers of

WEIGHING THE DEMONIC

The devil and demons are very prominent in Matthew, Mark and Luke. The Epistles talk little of the devil and not at all of demons or deliverance. They reflect the Old Testament's reticence about the demonic. What are the implications of this variety within Scripture – which corresponds to a variety of attitudes about the demonic among Christians today?

- Is it that there are a number of non-material evil beings regularly active in the world, but not everyone is sensitive to them?
- Is it that there are a number of such beings, but they vary the pattern of their activity? So they may be more active in some contexts and cultures than others.
- Is it that the Bible simply has several ways of describing evil, and it doesn't much matter which 'model' we accept?

One implication of the variety is that there are things to learn both from the personal and the impersonal ways of speaking about evil. Evil involves forces and structures, as well as being embodied from time to time in people like Peter.

The issue of the demonic must also be worked out in the awareness that, in the life and death of Jesus, the great battle between God and evil was played out. Jesus' battle with evil does not mean that *we* too have to fight one – it means he has fought it once and for all already. What we have to do is enter into the fruits of his victory.

the saints were the realm's protection.

- When people used to take their stand at the highest point in the parish on Ascension Day and hail the day that saw Jesus rise, they were declaring his lordship over the pagan worship which was once carried on at these highest places.

Defence and attack

Our enemy the devil prowls around like a roaring lion seeking someone to devour, but we are to resist him (1 Peter 5:8-9). For such a confrontation, we need armour (Ephesians 6:10-18). The hymn *St Patrick's Breastplate* reminds us of all that we 'bind to ourselves' in this fight. Sacramental confession is a natural preparation for deliverance ministry, to ensure that we have said sorry and got right with God before engaging in the spiritual battle.

Among the objects of our attack are our own inner 'demons' (see 2 Corinthians 10:3-5; 1 Thessalonians 5:22). For this we need other people's prayers, asking for the Spirit to burn away the evil inside. The declaring of the Creed also constitutes a standing firm and saying 'This is what I am' in the context of the battle. The repeating of choruses such as *He is Lord,* and the use of the sign of the cross, have similar significance.

Bearing suffering

Handling suffering is part of spiritual warfare (2 Timothy 2:3). Undue self-confidence can be our downfall, so a 'thorn in the flesh' may protect us (2 Corinthians 12:7-10). What Satan intended as a message from him functions in the opposite way. The obverse of the prosperity gospel and the 'name it and claim it' theory is the awareness that weakness means strength. Fighting the devil is costly.

Guardian angels?

It is silly to think that demons are the only significant heavenly beings. Our angels are always looking into the face of our Father in heaven and so reminding our Father of us (Matthew 18:10); and they are active on earth on our behalf too (if not always as spectacularly as in Acts 12:7-10). We worship 'with angels and archangels', part of a great company of heaven.

HOW GOD ACTS

All the issues raised in this Unit involve the question of how God relates to the world. The charismatic movement emphasises that God is involved in our world. The world is not a closed system which God may have created but now leaves to run itself. God intervenes.

That conviction needs setting in the context of a broader understanding of God's involvement in the world. Exercising irresistible power is one of God's ways of acting: Jesus' miracles illustrate it. They justify us in praying for miracles. But:

- God also acts by interaction with human beings, by convincing people to do things.
- God acts through the process of cause and effect built into the working of the universe and of human life (so if we are healthier spiritually, we should be healthier physically).
- God acts by means of human decisions which people make without reference to God but which God utilizes so that they contribute to the divine purpose.

Charismatic thinking easily talks as if only the first of these really counts as God's acting. Non-charismatic thinking easily thinks of God as the divine watchmaker who wound the world up and set it going but now leaves it to itself.

THE SPIRIT AND THE CROSS

I once had to speak at a weekend on 'inter-faith' questions. For me one of the most interesting features was listening to someone giving her testimony to her 'new age' spirituality. Its emphases on matters such as healing, the intuitive and openness, corresponded point by point to the emphases of charismatic spirituality. What made her unable to identify with Christianity (she said) was Good Friday and the emphasis on the death of Christ.

The great strength and the fatal weakness of charismatic spirituality is its emphasis on Pentecost, if that is not systematically linked to Good Friday.

And how God speaks

We really do not know for certain what any of the speaking gifts were in New Testament times: this is true of prophecy, tongues, 'interpretation', and words of wisdom and knowledge. Yet this need not inhibit our openness to God's speaking.

I assume that whatever these gifts were in New Testament times, they were examples of God speaking in appropriate ways to particular cultures. Even if we knew exactly what they were, the way God speaks in our culture might need to be very different. A key fact about gifts is that they work via the intuitive rather than the analytic – which may be one reason why women are often more open to them than men. Their challenge for us in the body of Christ is to put analytic and intuitive together.

If we expect that God should speak now, this raises questions regarding the relationship of this with God's message in Scripture. Before the charismatic movement, we were told that gifts such as prophecy were confined to biblical times. We have the Bible, so the gifts are no longer manifested. A lovely fruit of Roman Catholic charismatic renewal has been a budding and flowering of interest in Scripture. But within evangelicalism, Scripture is less important in renewal circles than it once was.

As with God 'acting', we need to hold different truths together. God *spoke*; and God *speaks*. We need to listen to both.

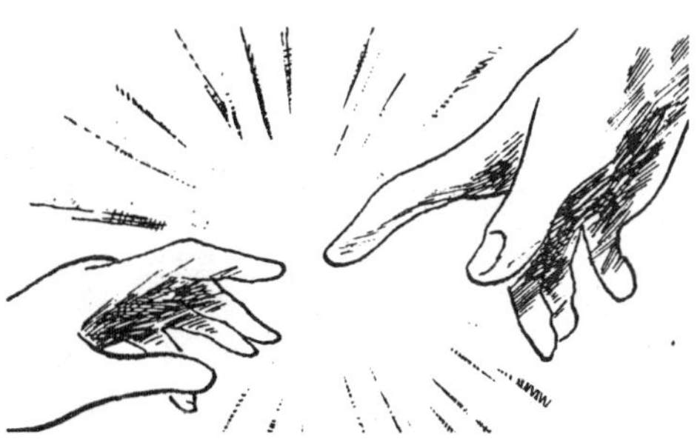

Unit **5**

AND SO TO PRAYER

PURPOSE

This Unit discusses one of the most common uses of prayer, but perhaps the least understood – prayer to God for other people, or intercession.

If you have struggled with missionary prayer letters, agonized over unanswered prayers, or puzzled about what is really going on when we pray that God will do things that will otherwise not happen, then this Unit may help you to pray with greater understanding – and conviction.

CONTENTS

TALKING TO GOD ABOUT OTHERS

What is prayer?

It's an odd thing about English that we have special words for prayer – prayer, petition, supplication, intercession – words that we rarely use outside a religious context. In Hebrew and Greek you use ordinary everyday words. Spoken prayer is simply talking to God. The words you use for the various aspects of prayer are words which mean 'say thank you', 'say sorry', 'ask for something', 'wish', 'mention', for yourself or on behalf of someone else.

These ordinary words help us to see the nature of prayer. It is having the kind of conversation with God which naturally arises out of the fact that God is a person and so are we.

In the narrowest sense 'prayer' implies asking for things from God, for ourselves or for other people. In a broader sense 'prayer' covers all ways of talking to God. In a broader sense still, 'prayer' covers all ways of relating to God and can include lots of silence, listening, and just being together with God.

Intercession (asking for things for someone else) is one of the forms of spoken prayer. It is unselfish prayer, a way of loving others, a natural and inevitable result of love.

Intercession desires for other people more than it is within our power to give them.

MY UNDERSTANDING OF INTERCESSION

by Florence

Intercession consists of three major acts:

- sorrow, burden, concern
- desire to see change
- action or prayer.

To intercede, for me, involves a great burden that I feel for a particular person, place, or issue. Sometimes that is laid on my heart by the Spirit of God when I know little about the person concerned or when I have not met a person. At other times it could start with a little experience or a story about the experience of a particular person which I consider very important, or which suggests something which needs changing. This lingers in my heart and I feel committed to praying to see a change in it. For instance, since I came to England from Nigeria I have been carrying a burden to pray for the Church of England and for the country, even though I know little about either.

In intercession I am standing with the person or issue. My intercessory spirit leads me to thinking about what I could do, and starting to do it. I pray about it regularly or daily. Sometimes I fast because of it. It seems to me that where there is no burden for the particular issue and desire to see change, there may never develop an intercessory spirit. We hear, desire, and act (in fervent prayer, keeping vigil, and fasting if necessary, and listening to what the Spirit of God may be leading us to do). The prayer is not for a short period, but until God responds.

Some questions

Here are some common questions that I have heard asked about intercession:

- How does faith relate to intercession (e.g. healings in the gospels)?
- What is the link with spiritual warfare?
- Why repeat prayers?
- How much is breadth important, and how much is depth (e.g. praying a bit for all the world or a lot for one country)?
- How do you pray for situations you don't know?
- How do you lead intercessions in church? Is there a difference between individual and community intercessions?
- Why do people pray for the dead?
- What is the role of Jesus in intercession?
- What kind of parent gives children what is good for them only if they beg often or long enough?
- Does prayer change God's mind?
- How can you reconcile opposed intercessions?
- How do you pray for people you don't like?
- Can you back-date prayers?

What questions would *you* like to add? Put some here...

✎

Some assumptions

In *What Are We Doing When We Pray?*, Vincent Brümmer suggests that when we pray we (rightly) presuppose the following:

- God can choose whether or not to do things.
- God sometimes only does things when asked.
- God can have a change of mind – although remaining consistent and faithful.
- God knows all possible futures but relates to us in the present.
- God already knows what we want but wants to live in relationship with us, which means that we need to say what we want.
- In prayer we are making ourselves available to God to use in the fulfilment of the divine purpose.
- God may occasionally work by 'breaking natural laws' but more often works by utilizing the inbuilt indeterminacy in nature.
- God can work through human beings without overriding their freedom, by providing the circumstances or the inspiration that make some acts possible.

Do you share all these assumptions? Which would you question? Mark them on the list. Would you want to add others? Write them here...

✎

'When we move from petition to intercession we are shifting our centre of gravity from our own needs to the needs and concerns of others'

Richard Forster, *Prayer*, p. 203

THE BIBLE AND INTERCESSION

It is striking that the *way* we pray, and *what* we pray, for other people, is often very different from the way people pray in Scripture or the content of *their* prayer for others.

Look up the references below and write down how Scripture encourages us to pray for others:

WHAT AND HOW TO PRAY

• for the people of God
Exodus 32-34, Nehemiah 1, Luke 23:34, John 17, Ephesians 1:15-23, 3:14-19, Philippians 1:9-11, Colossians 1:3-14, 1 Thessalonians 3:12-13, 5:23-24

• for a disciple, evangelist, missionary or minister
Luke 22:31-32, Romans 15:30-32, Ephesians 6:18-20, Colossians 4:2-4

• for governments and nations
Genesis 18:22-33, Psalm 20, Psalm 72, 1 Timothy 2:1-7

• for someone in need
Psalms 5, 6, 13, 22, 25, 27, 31, 32, 42-43, 63

Try it!

Start with five minutes of quiet:

- Don't worry about not knowing how to pray; remember the Holy Spirit prays for you and in you; be encouraged (Romans 8:26-27).
- Think of yourself as welcomed into God's presence because Jesus intervened for you (Hebrews 7:25).

Then for (say) fifteen minutes:

- Take a Bible passage about what people pray for the people of God (e.g. Ephesians 3:14-19), and imagine what it would be like for that to be fulfilled for a church or a Christian group you pray for. Picture it to God. Ask God to bring it about.
- Do the same with a passage about what people pray for disciples/ministers/missionaries/evangelists (e.g. Ephesians 6:18-20), on behalf of someone you know (e.g. someone in your church).
- Do the same with a passage regarding a government or nation (e.g. Psalm 72).
- Do the same with a Psalm of lament (e.g. Psalm 6) on behalf of someone present or someone you know or know of.

Each time

- Think of yourself as having a meeting with God on someone's behalf. See yourself standing before God to speak for them.
- Think of things to thank God for with regard to the object of your prayer, and give thanks.
- Tell God what is going on and challenge God about it.

Clues from the Gospels

Look at Matthew 7-9 to see what it implies about intercession. Choose at least three of the sections below to read and reflect on.

7:7-11 Getting what you ask for
8:1-3 What does *God* want?
8:5-13 What faith is
8:14-15 Answer without a question?
8:16-17 The role of Jesus
8:23-27 The size of faith
8:28-34 A price to pay?
9:1-8 Sin in the way?
9:18-19, 23-26 It's ridiculous!
9:20-22 Just a touch of faith
9:27-31 Do you believe?
9:32-34 Whose power at work?
9:35-38 Driven by pity

Write down particular things you have learned from these passages.

Now spend fifteen minutes praying for other people on the basis of what you have learned!

THE LORD'S PRAYER

How might each of the petitions of the Lord's Prayer relate to intercession? Use the Lord's Prayer for intercession in the light of what you discover.

A BIBLE STUDY

Choose one of the passages below:

- Genesis 18:17-33 (Abraham praying for Sodom)
- Exodus 32:7-14 (Moses praying for Israel)
- Jeremiah 14:1-12 (Jeremiah forbidden to pray for Israel)
- Ephesians 1:15-23 (Paul praying for the Ephesian church)

Then ask yourself the following questions:

- What do you learn about intercession from the passage?

- How does it contradict what we usually think about intercession?

- What differences does it imply for your interceding?

- What encouragement does it give for your interceding?

MY APPROACH TO INTERCESSION

by Andrew

Only being a beginner at intercessory prayer, I see it as standing in someone's place and interceding for them or for a situation, to the Lord. I often find it difficult and I struggle, particularly when a situation seems hopeless, but I suppose that's part of it – just keeping on in spite of the situation or myself. I find myself interceding for friends, family, local, national, and international issues, and often at times more fervently than at others. I believe we ought to intercede whether or not we feel like it, though there can be great joy when the Lord answers, so thanksgiving mustn't be forgotten.

THE LOGIC OF INTERCESSION

Intercession no doubt implies that we commit ourselves to implement God's decisions – but it must not be watered down to a form of prayer whose real significance is to change <u>us</u>.

If we want to understand intercession Abraham is an important example because he is the Bible's first intercessor (see Genesis 18:17-33).

God chooses to involve us

God revealed to Abraham the judgment that was to come on Sodom – and waited to discover his response. This led Abraham to challenge God about how this judgment was to implemented. Surely the judge of all the earth must do what is right? God agreed to see that the judgment was executed in a just way.

God gave Abraham a share in the decision-making process. Abraham shared God's responsibility to see that right prevailed in the world.

Here is a pattern which often appears in scripture. It begins with God announcing an intention, but then (strangely) not putting the intention into effect. It all depends on what goes on between God and the people. Prayers such as Abraham's come in the 'gap' between the announcement of divine intentions and their subsequent fulfilment.

For more about this pattern, see S E Balentine, *Prayer in the Hebrew Bible* (Augsberg Fortress Publishers, 1993) pages 39-40

Abraham is God's means of realizing the purpose of creation, which failed in Genesis 1-11. His role in Genesis 18 is part of that. It presupposes a fundamental aspect of the way God relates to all of us human beings. God created us Godlike, and commissioned us to share in God's running of the world (Genesis 1:26). Intercession is an integral part of human life as God created it.

Prayers of blessing (and cursing) can be seen as 'relatives' of prayers of intercession. They presuppose that God has delegated authority to human beings. That is why our words can have the power and effectiveness of God's own words.

A prophet's role

Abraham is the first prophet in the Bible, and is considered a prophet *because* he is an intercessor (Genesis 20:7). Intercession was integral to prophecy:

- **Samuel** saw it as a sin against Yahweh if he stopped praying for God's people (1 Samuel 12:23).
- **Amos'** job is to query whether judgment really should be implemented (Amos 7)
- **Moses'** conversation with God in Exodus 32-34 illustrates the same reality (compare God's regret in Ezekiel 22:30).
- **Jeremiah** 14-15 proves the rule, as Jeremiah is *forbidden* to intercede in order to get a decision changed and thus cannot fulfil the normal role of a prophet.

Praying for mercy and forgiveness for people is of decisive importance to what actually happens to them. The intercessions of prophets ensure that people do not pay the full penalty for their failures.

Prophets are admitted to Yahweh's cabinet (Jeremiah 23:18). This puts prophets in a position to prophesy, but it also enables them to take part in the deliberations of the cabinet – and to question plans announced by God. Prophets use their position to urge God to take mercy seriously, just as they urge people to take God's wrath seriously. Thus prophets are identified with both parties and with neither – which is why their role is uncomfortable and isolated.

God in the chair

We often think of God as like an ancient monarch, one who exercises absolute power. God is also seen as a father who wants what is best for his children. Such pictures are scriptural ones, but they are not the whole truth. The Bible also implies another picture which needs combining with these.

God is like the chair of a meeting, or a shop-steward at a union meeting, or a (half-decent) vicar. A vicar does not decide alone on parish policies and then implement them, but involves the people of the parish in the *process* of decision-making and implementation. Similarly, God does not act alone, but collaboratively.

We have seen God's way of doing this with the prophets. It can also be seen in the general story of the Old and New Testaments and in the story of the Church. It is clear from those stories that God does not impose a *will* but seeks to draw people into the fulfilment of the divine *purpose* (usually failing). God's purpose embraces the process – it requires the involvement of people. Intercession is one way we take part in the process whereby decisions are taken and implemented.

So the chair, the shop steward and the vicar reflect God's way of setting about the implementing of a purpose. Of course a vicar will have some *aims* with regard to areas such as evangelism and worship, will keep working at those, and ultimately will not give up on them. But the way and the timing may be endlessly negotiable, because *the process is part of the aim*. The kind of community the vicar is committed to building has to be involved in the fulfilment of the aims, otherwise the vicar's aims will not be fulfilled.

In a parallel way, God has some ultimate aims (e.g. that people come to know God, that right comes to prevail in the world), and our prayer needs to accord with God's will in the sense of matching those aims. But because of that concern for process and the building of a community, God is willing to be tirelessly flexible about the fulfilment of these aims.

To intercede, then, is to urge that certain decisions get taken and implemented on the basis of their consistency with the aims. If we do not take part in this urging, then decisions may not get taken in the way we wanted. The discussions are real, and they issue in real change.

At least they *may* do so. There is no mystery about the fact that many of our contributions to the debate, many of our urgings, do not win assent. There are other insights and other factors that overcome them this time. Perhaps another time this will not be so; so it is worth keeping making our point, because its moment may come.

And when we intervene with an 'Amen' in the midst of someone's prayer, it is like saying 'Yes' or nodding our head when someone makes a contribution to a debate. It adds to the force of the argument. Likewise when we pray 'in Jesus' name' we are claiming that the point we make is in conformity with Jesus' priorities; that too adds to the force of the argument (see John 14:13-14, 15:7,16, 16:23-24).

Angels also belong to Yahweh's cabinet, and take part in its deliberations by interceding for us and for the world (see Zechariah 3).

A CHANGE OF MIND?

When the chair of a meeting advocates a course of action, this is really a *proposal* not a decision. It is a matter for people to debate, and the debate may lead to a different course of action from the one proposed. In the light of the debate the chair will be free to have a change of mind about what should be done, even if this implies no change of mind about ultimate aims. To change one's mind in that context is a sign of strength.

In the same way the Bible assumes that God is free to have a change of mind in the course of equivalent discussions. As we have seen, OT intercession is characteristically designed to change the chair's mind, about a decision concerning the world (Genesis 18) or concerning the people of God (Exodus 32-34).

ON BEHALF OF THE HELPLESS

It is characteristic of group deliberations that people speak urgently and fervently on behalf of groups they represent, especially those who cannot represent themselves.

This is also so with intercession. To intercede involves standing in the place of people who need to have their position represented (compare the 'as though' in Hebrews 13:3). So intercession may involve praying the Psalms of lament on behalf of people oppressed or hurting, and urging God to meet their need in a way they may not feel able to do themselves.

Thus in intercession we may pray for 'us' rather than for 'them' (see Jeremiah 14:19-22). The prayers of the Psalms are capable of moving between 'I' and 'they' as the intercessor oscillates between identification and distinction (e.g. Psalm 3). Isaiah 62:6-7 offers another picture of this – here pressing for decisions already made to be implemented.

Romans 8:26-27 sees the Spirit as *our* intercessor, while Romans 8:34 and Hebrews 7:25 see Christ as our intercessor in the manner of an OT priest. Christ or the Spirit makes meetings between us and God possible. Christ does that *objectively* – it is because Christ died for us that we have the right to re-join the meeting where decisions are made, and to speak there (another way of understanding prayer 'in the name of Jesus'). The Spirit does it *subjectively*, giving us the confidence to speak, the ideas and words to speak, and the instinct for what is in accordance with God's nature.

Intercession (praying for others) is the same as supplication (praying for yourself) except that you are doing it *as if* you were someone else, doing it *for* someone else. So however you pray for yourself, do that with other people in mind. Prayer for ourselves starts from *our* helplessness and gives God access to our needs (Revelation 3:20). In intercession we identify with someone else's helplessness and give God access to *their* needs.

Putting up a fight

Intervening and arguing a case may involve effort and persistence. This is one reason why prayer can be hard work. There may be no special reason why we find it difficult to give intercession the doggedness it requires – other than the usual reasons why we avoid hard work and give in before tasks are completed! It simply raises questions about discipline. The NT's stress on persistence and perseverance in prayer (e.g. Romans 12:12, Colossians 4:2) perhaps suggests that there is nothing modern about the difficulty we have in this.

Paul speaks of prayer as engaging in a fight (Romans 15:30, Colossians 2:1, 4:12). For people such as Abraham, and Moses at Sinai, the battle of prayer is a struggle with God, a battle to change God's mind. But for Moses in Exodus 17, it is a

INTERVENERS?

The (rare) OT word *'paga'*, translated 'intercede' (Isaiah 53:12; Jeremiah 7:16; 15:11) means in ordinary speech to 'meet' or 'intervene' (Genesis 23:8; Ruth 1:16 NRSV 'press'; Isaiah 59:16). An intercessor is one who intervenes and has a meeting with another person on someone's behalf.

THANKSGIVING

In intervening on someone's behalf, we sometimes need to commend them as worth acting on behalf of. So in praying to God there is a close relationship between thanksgiving and intercession (e.g. Philippians 1:3-5).

In thanksgiving we draw attention to what God has already achieved in people's lives, which is a reason for God's work in them to be taken further.

matter of exercising authority over forces which themselves battle against God's people. In Ephesians 6, too, it is a battle against other powers.

In battling to change God's mind we assume there is another side to God to appeal to. In battling against other powers we assume we can appeal to God as the chair of the group.

Being priests and prophets

In the Old Testament, intercession is the task of the prophet and the priest. Arguably the priest makes it *possible* (by helping to restore people's relationship with Yahweh) and the prophet makes it *actual* (by actually interceding and getting God's agreement).

If the Church is filled by the Spirit of prophecy and inherits the priesthood of Christ, it is the Church's task to take its part in the process of decision-making and representation by being involved in intercession. If all believers may prophesy and may approach God's presence, it follows that all may share in the process of intercession. Indeed, for them *not* to do so has the same snags as when some people never take part in a discussion in a meeting – the decisions are then taken only on the basis of the arguments of those who were willing to speak.

At the same time, if some have a special gift of prophecy or a special position as priests, it follows that some have a special gift or responsibility for intercession. Paul's intercession is an aspect of his exercise of a priestly ministry. Part of his responsibility for the churches in his care was to present them to Christ whole, holy, and mature, when he appears (see Romans 15:15-16).

INTERCESSION AND TEMPERAMENT

In their book *Prayer and Temperament*, C. P. Michael and M. C. Norrisey apply the Myers-Briggs personality profile to prayer in a general way, working with four basic personality types (without considering intercession in particular).

SJ Sensing/judging.

People such as: James, Matthew, Ignatius.

Conservative, stresses duty. Emphasizes recollection of past events which makes them present now. SJs have a deep sense of obligation, want to give rather than receive, are pessimistic, good at organization. This kind of prayer is structured and orderly but makes much use of the imagination to enter into scriptural scenes.

NF Intuitive/feeling.

People such as: Paul, Luke, Augustine.

Visionary, person-oriented, creative, optimistic, communicate easily, enthusiastic, concerned to grow, keen for future possibilities, like symbols, prayer stones and candles, quiet and meditation, tears. They also use the imagination, but to seek to let scripture speak now.

SP Sensing/perceiving.

People such as: Peter, Mark, Francis.

'Free spirit', activist. Impulsive, living in present, intense, celebratory, contacting God through the visible, audible, tangible, and using arts and crafts. Like prayer walks and arrow-prayers arising out of contexts.

NT Intuition/thinking.

People such as: John, Thomas Aquinas.

Mystic, likes ideas, logical, perfectionist, competitive, self-disciplined, orderly, reflecting discursively on concepts, stressing orderly movement of thought in the relationship of cause and effect, thirsting for truth.

Can you apply these temperament types to intercession? What approaches to intercession might different types find natural?

TEARS FOR OTHERS

In Scripture and in Christian history, tears have been a natural part of praying for other people and for oneself. They vividly express the complex interweaving of body, spirit, feelings, mind and subconscious.

In the Psalms people draw attention to their tears. If we are hurt, the Psalms assume that the natural thing is to cry; and if we are hurt before God, we cry before God and expect God to notice, as a child cries before its mother and expects her to notice (see Psalm 39:12, 56:8).

Individuals and cultures differ about how easily they weep. In Western cultures some people have been taught not to cry; others have a hard time restraining their tears. 'The gift of tears' invites us to see tears as inspired by the Spirit, perhaps parallel to tongues. It is a gift which expresses our prayer for others in a physical way, and may free them to express their own hurt or joy.

A key aspect of intercession is putting ourselves in the place of someone else and praying as if we are that person. We do that when we weep in prayer for others.

Weeping our tears and discovering what they mean may be part of acknowledging hurts and sins from which we have hidden, and may thus help us find forgiveness and healing.

The wiping away of tears

We cannot have the joy of prayer answered without praying some prayers. So we cannot have the joy of tears wiped away without having shed some (see Luke 6:21). If we have shed tears, then we can prove that those who sow in tears (not believing that there can ever be a harvest again, that the laughter of the past can ever be laughter in the present) do reap in joy (Psalm 126). And we can know that the sending of disaster which caused tears is not God's last word (see Isaiah 25:8, taken up in Revelation 7:17, 21:4).

Jesus' ministry shows that this wiping away of tears is not an experience for which we necessarily have to wait until the End. He acts on behalf of the weeping widow at Nain and therefore she can stop weeping (Luke 7:13). He asks Mary Magdalene why she is weeping and in addressing her by name wipes away her tears (John 20:11-16). At Bethany he tells people they have no need to weep, after first allowing himself to be drawn into their weeping (John 11:31-35).

OVER THE TOP?

'All night long I flood my bed with weeping and drench my couch with tears' (Psalm 6.6) or 'crying has been my food and drink' (Psalm 42.3) may seem to be laying it on a bit thick, but are perhaps no more an exaggeration than 'I cried my eyes out'.

TEARS AND LOVE

Tears are strange things. The person who most clearly reveals an emotional love for Jesus does so with tears (Luke 7:38).

JEREMIAH

Jeremiah was once referred to as the 'weeping prophet', and that was something he himself wanted to be. He wanted to overflow unceasingly with tears for the sake of his own people because of the loss which their own sin had put them through and which threatened to put them through more loss (see Jeremiah 9:1, 14:17). His tears accompany his pleading with God not to cast the people off, not to act as if despising them, not to keep afflicting them like the oppressors observed by Ecclesiastes, not to abandon the covenant relationship with the people (14:19-21).

Jeremiah's tears also accompany his verbalizing on their behalf the confession of sin which is needed if God is to heed that prayer (14:20). Those tears over their sin are shed in their stead (they are tears they should shed). Other tears at their sin are shed because of his own grief at that sin and his awareness of where it will lead (13:17). Paul similarly weeps over the enemies of the cross of Christ (Philippians 3:18). The solemnity of the issues in a parallel way makes Paul weep when he faces people with ultimate issues in his preaching (Acts 2:19,31, 2 Corinthians 4:4).

When Jeremiah's preaching is not heard, neither are his prayers, and in due course the city has to do its own weeping before God for its children (Lamentations 2:11, 18-19).

When Jesus wept over the city of Jerusalem, he takes up Jeremiah's ministry (Luke 19:41-44).

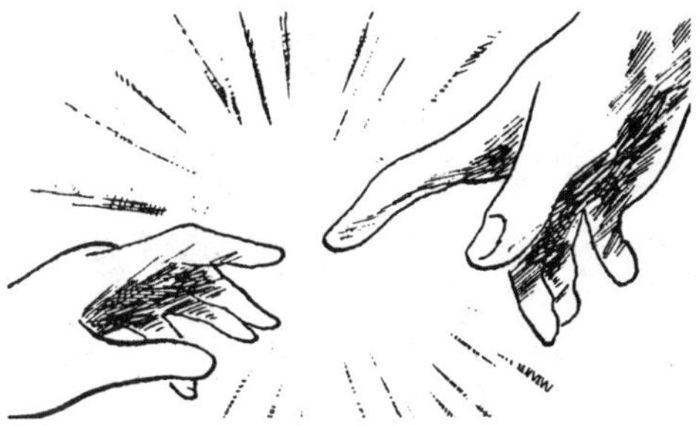

Unit 6

SKILLS FOR THE JOURNEY

PURPOSE

This Unit is about 'spiritual disciplines', things we can do to help ourselves make progress in our spiritual lives. They are called 'disciplines' because they are hard work and require concentrated effort.

We all need such help – the greatest saints have seen that most clearly. Here is an opportunity to turn your good intentions into actual change in your life with God.

CONTENTS

NOT SLAVES BUT SERVANTS

In general, you achieve very little in life if you don't put some effort in. The spiritual life is no exception.

The various ways of concentrating our efforts to achieve spiritual goals for ourselves, are called the 'spiritual disciplines'. Traditionally they are things like fasting, confession, solitude and meditation.

There are two traps in thinking about spiritual disciplines.

- One is to **avoid** thinking about the issue – to see the Christian life as God offering us self-fulfilment by loving us and accepting us as we are, so what is the need for effort?
- The other is get **preoccupied** with the issue – and turn the freedom of the Christian life into another form of bondage.

The first of these traps is the more contemporary one; more Christians fall into it than would have been the case 40 years ago. But the kind of people who study a course on spirituality are as likely to fall into the second...

Living our lives for God involves us in disciplined service. To get the discipline right, we have to understand the nature of the service:

Serving God is a response

We are saved by God's grace, and our service is a response to what God has done for us. We know this at head level but at gut level we often believe we will only be acceptable on the basis of our achievements. We know we live by grace, but how many of us are doing it?

The insights we have considered from Romans 6 are key here (see pages 28-29). We were slaves to sin, guilt and death. It was not merely that we *felt* in bondage but that we had actually become under obligation to serve them. But Christ died for us. That ended our obligation. They continue to con us that they still control us, but factually they have no authority or rights in respect of us now. We are free. We *can* serve God freely now.

'Our obedience is shaped, authorised and limited by our imagination. Therefore if we are to have changed obedience, we must have transformed imagination'
W. Brueggemann, ***Interpretation and Obedience***

We *must* also do so. 'The God who liberates is also the one who sets the terms for a human future... [The ten commandments] set the perimeters for new life that is neither oppressively conformist nor unrealistically autonomous.' (W. Brueggemann, *Interpretation and Obedience* page 147)

Serving God means saying 'Yes'

Christian service involves saying yes to things you really don't want to do. (Generally it's OK in the end, but are you allowed to bank on that?)

In Hebrew, 'service', 'slavery' and 'worship' are the same word. We like singing 'The servant king' but it is another matter living it. An older generation sang 'All to Jesus I surrender' – and often meant it. 19th century evangelicalism saw some significant sacrifices made for God, and it wasn't all legalism.

A clergyman I know applied for a parish job he expected to get but didn't want. He applied because he knew what urgently needed doing in that parish and knew he could do it. (To his surprise he didn't get it.)

Serving God can be enormously fulfilling, and God cares for us in it. God honours it when we pay the cost. No matter how much we give, God always gives us more back. But Christian service is not primarily a means of self-fulfilment.

Those who work in the church can find it hard to say 'No', because they always want to say 'Yes' to God. They may find it helpful to think in terms of what they are under obligation to a *system* to do, and what they do for *God* as a free act of servant's love. One clergy tutor at St John's says he works for college a certain number of hours a week as an obligation, for which he gets paid. He then works some more hours for God (e.g. preaching on Sundays) as part of his free servant's response to God.

It is one thing to write a blank cheque for God to fill in the amount – but quite another to let the Church get to it before God can.

Ordinand: 'Look what it cost me to offer for the ministry.'

Jesus: 'Look what it cost me.'

Serving God encourages greater maturity

One warm Sunday evening in September 1965 we were walking home from church, discussing the vicar (as one does). I commented that it was a shame he was so brusque. My wife said, 'But you're the same.' 'No I'm not,' I said. But she pointed to something which had just happened which illustrated it.

Christian service involves letting who you are and what you do be given over to God's service and thus refined and sanctified. Each aspect of you (especially the weaknesses) is a potential strength when given over to God. Each aspect of you (especially your strengths) is a potential weakness when not.

We are also called to be servants of one another. I wonder if we need to develop amongst us a culture of encouragement or affirmation, as co-servants of a gracious Master.

I heard an archdeacon comment that when he does appraisals for parish clergy, he spends all the time encouraging them because they are so ground down through being got at or treated as slaves by their congregations. It's not just true for clergy.

Jesus us calls us to exercise a love that is 'perfect' – fully grown-up, mature (Mat 5:48). How about covenanting to exercise a servant's ministry of encouragement to one another?

'Maturity is a compound of wisdom, goodwill, resilience, and creativity.'

J. I. Packer, *The Quest for Godliness*

BRINGING ORDER INTO LIFE

'I haven't the time'. Most of us use the phrase. Somehow the hours, days and weeks go by, and we haven't done the things we really wanted to do.

It may be that we have huge demands on our time: I think of single parents I know who have to juggle children, work, church, shopping, looking after a house... Yet even people whose lives look simpler feel that time just disappears without anything to show for it. We are often driven by other people's agendas.

In one sense, being in control of your own life is one way of defining of sin – it implies running our own lives independently of God's purposes. But in another sense it is an aspect of 'wisdom', the nearest Old Testament word for 'spirituality'.

In spirituality we talk of developing a 'rule of life'. The aim of a rule of life is to help us get control of our lives – rather than be controlled by them, by other people, and by their pressures. It's about our lives being under the control of us and God, rather than being controlled by other people and the god of this age.

It's a bit like financial planning. If you know where the money needs to go (and where it is actually going!), you are more likely to be able to get a grip of your finances. You can then plan to do sensible and godly things with your money. As we seek to be good stewards of our money, so we seek to be good stewards of our time.

So a 'rule of life' is about planning your time. It's about *you* deciding where the time should go, so that you can live your life as God's person, rather than as driven by other people's demands or by your own weakness.

Starting from facts

I have a colleague who regularly fills in a chart so that he can show where each half-hour of the day goes. He works for more than one boss, and also has work-goals outside the 9am-5pm confines of office hours. Keeping his chart helps him look bosses in the eye ('I am doing as much as I should' or 'You are asking of me more than you should'), and he can also see for himself where the time is going and look for specific ways he can change things.

You might like to do that for a week or two as background for what follows. These are some of the categories you might need:

- employment or other work
- family and home responsibilities
- church
- prayer
- relaxation and leisure
- practical service of people
- sleeping and eating

You may want to add some others.

Before you fill in the chart, you might want to decide what you *wish* the proportions were, and to guess what the proportions *actually* are – and then compare your wishes and your guesses with your findings...

What you will discover is that you already have a rule of life or a pattern of life. Once you know it, you can change it.

DOES GOD MIND?

New year resolutions are a joke. Most people fail to keep most of them. Most resolutions to eat less chocolate or give up smoking get no-one anywhere.

So it is with our rule of life – and that can be disheartening. We may get discouraged by our failures. That is the point at which to ask, 'If I were God, would I mind that so-and-so hasn't managed to keep up their rule of life?' The answer is probably 'No'. Most of us are harder on ourselves than we would be on other people.

It is also perhaps the time to ask, 'Is my rule of life unrealistic, or was that failure just a blip?' and 'Are there things I should do to make the rule work?'

Making an outline plan

You now need to come up with a realistic plan. The word 'realistic' is important! While part of our problem in being disciplined is ourselves, part of it is the real constraints upon us. You have to start from where you are.

When people are concerned about where the time goes, they often feel guilty or sad about the time they spend in prayer (or rather, *don't* spend in prayer…). You could take that question first. Suppose you want to spend (say) 15 minutes of quality time with God per day. Look at your day as a whole and decide when and where that can be. If that is a priority you want to make, you need to fit that in *first* and then fit in other things round it, rather than the other way round.

- Maybe you are awake first thing in the morning, and could find the time then over a cup of coffee for you and God to look at the day ahead, make plans, make commitments, and for you to ask for God's help.
- Or maybe you would prefer it to be last thing at night over a cup of chocolate (or a glass of port…), when you and God can look over the day together and assess, reflect, interpret, be thankful, confess, cry, laugh, rage.
- Or maybe it will be 15 minutes when the baby has a lie down.
- Or 15 minutes in a church during your lunch hour.
- Or (write your own) ……………… ………………………………………

Christians sometimes feel that their church activities take up too much time compared with family time and involvement in the world. If so, decide when family times will be, and how you would like to be involved in the world – and what church activities you will cut. If you are attached to what you do in the church, this last bit will hurt. So do it quickly – like taking a plaster off a wound.

Broadening the plan

Are there other things you would like to fit into your life each week? For instance:

- worship
- Bible study
- keeping a spiritual journal
- reading a book
- fasting
- rest, relaxation, and exercise
- exercising hospitality

Then there are things that do not come about every week. You may want to think whether want to programme in:

- a quiet day
- a retreat
- a meeting of a mutual guidance group or with a spiritual director (see pages 80-81)
- confession
- personal review and assessment (including reviewing your rule)

It helps to take account of the Church's year and your observance of Advent, Christmas, Lent, Holy Week/Easter, and Pentecost.

TV ADDICTS?

You may have to face the fact that you watch too much TV. If so, decide what programmes to watch – and determine whether and when you will ever switch on 'just to see what's on' (I sometimes do that at 10pm if I think it will help me wind down).

You might like to try a grid like this in which to incorporate the various elements of life with God we have mentioned.

Contexts of our life with God

Time flow	Individual	Group	Church	Family	Daily life
Daily					
Weekly					
Monthly					
Annually					

HOW TO USE SILENCE

MEDITATION

The terms 'meditation' and 'contemplation' are used in a variety of different ways. Sometimes they are a very active business in which you work hard at seeking to enter into a Bible passage. Sometimes they are an 'advanced' form of prayer which ordinary people may feel they never reach.

Here we are concerned with a form of prayer which is receptive rather than active and simple rather than technical – though it may take many of us a long time to come to it.

Sports programmes on television are noisier than they used to be. Goal-of-the-month compilations and the like are accompanied by thudding music as well as the traditional oohs and aahs. When eating in a restaurant this week, I noticed that the same music was being provided as 'background'. Theological Colleges often have an hour of 'quiet' each week, but increasing numbers of people find it hard to spend even one hour without words.

Silence in the Bible

We have seen that biblical prayer is usually noisy (see pages 16-17), and this is true whether it is praise, supplication or intercession. The Bible has no explicit 'silence ideal'. When people try to provide biblical texts for periods of silence, they are usually 'pre-texts'. The classic is 'Be still and know that I am God' (Psalm 46:10), which is not an invitation to contemplative prayer but a decisive command to people to stop engaging in battle and recognize that Yahweh is the great battler. 'Waiting' in the Bible involves waiting *for* God, waiting expectantly for God to act – not waiting *on* God, just being there in silence.

But Middle Eastern life two or three millennia ago was inherently quieter than modern Western life. The possibility of quiet could be taken for granted there. In those cultures, people no doubt had their ways of avoiding God and avoiding themselves, but noise was not one of them. They did however have to evade lengthy greetings in the street (see Luke 10:4), which could occupy you a long time. For us, stripping away noise may be a modern equivalent.

The prayer of silence is also the prayer of inactivity. We rightly see other forms of prayer (such as intercession) as hard work, as is Bible study and meditation. They have that disadvantage. In the prayer of silence we do – nothing. Although that is not work, it is hard for us in an activist age and an activist church.

A practical exercise

The basic idea is simple. God is with us. We do not have to go somewhere to be in God's presence; we *are* in God's presence. What we need is means of becoming aware of God's presence and being able to enjoy it – or perhaps being made to feel uncomfortable by it.

Go somewhere away from distraction. There is something to be

THE DISCIPLINE OF KNITTING

Anthony Bloom tells a story about silent prayer (see *School For Prayer*, pages 60-61). An old lady asked for advice about prayer. He told her to go to her room after breakfast, tidy it so that there is nothing that would worry her, and sit in her armchair. She was to light her candle before her icon, look round her room, and then knit for fifteen minutes before the face of God without saying one word of prayer. In doing so she became more and more aware of the silence, not an absence of something but a presence of something, with a density and a richness that began to pervade her. She told him later, 'All of a sudden I perceived that the silence was a presence. At the heart of the silence there was Him who is all stillness, all peace, all poise'.

He tells a similar story about a peasant who spent ages in a chapel doing nothing. Asked what he was doing, he explained, 'I look at Him, He looks at me, and we are happy'.

said for seeking God near the beginning of the day, when other things have had less chance to distract. But it may be more valuable to take time out from the pressures of the day; if so, the process of withdrawing may require more hard work. You may find it helpful (in imagination or in reality) to put things around you away – and disconnect the phone!

Sit in a comfortable position. You may value something as a focus for your eyes, such as a cross, a candle, an icon or a window over a garden (probably not a window over a busy street, though that might be good to stimulate intercession – another time!). Or you may prefer to shut your eyes; if you go to sleep for a while, take that as God's gift!

You may find an activity for your hands (such as knitting or drawing) a help. You may find music helpful. With many aspects of this, you have to find what works for you. I find music a distraction rather than a help, but I often have a cup of coffee.

Let body and mind unwind, relaxing muscles and imagining furrows falling from your brow (they will then do so!). Form a gentle smile, as if looking in the face of one you love (for that is what you are doing). And enjoy the presence of God for ten minutes (or five or thirty).

It is not necessarily a compromise of the notion of 'the prayer of silence' to use brief prayers, the kind that you can repeat over and over again. The classic is the Eastern Orthodox 'Jesus Prayer', 'Lord Jesus Christ, son of God, have mercy on me'. Or you can reduce it to the one word 'Jesus', like a lover naming their beloved. Or you can repeat scripture verses, perhaps ones which have been set to music such as 'Be still and know that I am God' (despite what I have said above). I find myself falling into the chorus 'Jesus we enthrone you'. And if I think of something I must remember to do something about, I write it down so that I can then forget about it again for the time being!

PRACTISING THE PRESENCE

In conjunction with realizing the presence of God at specific times, you can try reminding yourself of that presence at other times – waiting for the bus, walking down the street. After all, God is with us all the time, so we can be with God all the time.

You may also try going on a 'prayer walk' – adapting what has been described here to a walk with God. Or you could try having your time of silence in the bath. I have sorted things out with God in key ways on several occasions when driving a long way.

I expect there are people who go jogging with God, or play golf with God...

What will happen?

Perhaps nothing, which is fine. When two friends spend time with each other, it is not essential for anything to happen or anything to be said. You do not even have to have felt holy feelings for the time to have been 'worthwhile' or 'valid'. But you may well feel a quiet joy or awe at having spent time with God. You may find yourself:

- thinking things you have not thought before
- seeing a picture you have not seen before
- wanting to say something you have not said before
- weeping tears you have not wept before
- consumed by anger or guilt that you have not felt before
- compelled to go and do something you have not done before or face something you have not faced.

In due course, find a way of closing – by singing a chorus or saying the Lord's Prayer.

You may find yourself also studying the Bible, praying for yourself or for other people, giving thanks for what God has done for you, acknowledging your sins and seeking forgiveness, worshipping God, or wanting to write something in a 'prayer-journal'. But it is important for these not to take over the openness, inactivity and stillness involved in the prayer of silence. We are simply with God for God's sake.

When you have come to appreciate a bit of silence, then you can begin to appreciate a longer period of silence and solitude. That is the time to look for a quiet day or a longer retreat.

BEING QUIET WITH OTHERS

When we spend time in silence, we want Christ to be present with us. Jesus' promise about his presence is actually, 'Where two or three are gathered together, there am I in the midst.' So you can do exactly what I have described here in the company of a small group of other people, and afterwards share what has happened. It may be that God will give one person something to share which is for someone else.

FOSTERING A PASSION FOR GOD

Spiritual disciplines and religious commitment can sound like a lot of hard work. The Christian life is totally demanding, with God asking us always to be moving on, always serving others. Yet it is hugely fulfilling, and we often experience a sense of completeness in giving ourselves in this way.

So it is not surprising that many Christian people down the ages have seen a close parallel between a love for God and intimate human love. Lovers give everything, yet receive so much. They lose themselves, yet find themselves.

St John of the Cross

St John of the Cross was a mystic, a theologian and a church leader, in the Roman Catholic church in Spain in the period just after the Protestant Reformation. Soon after his birth in 1542 his father died and the family was reduced to poverty. But he was able to receive education, and at 20 felt called to join a religious order. He studied theology and was ordained at 24.

He then committed himself to the development and running of the reformed Carmelite order (at this point taking the name 'John of the Cross'). This involved him in ongoing conflicts within the church over the reform of the monastic system. When his 'branch' of the religious orders was legalized in 1580, he became responsible for much of its management, as Rector of the Carmelite college where he taught. During these ten years he did much of his writing. John became ill and died at 49 in 1591.

John's work comprises poems and prose. In these he suggests four images for the development of our life with God:

- falling in love (see *The Spiritual Canticle*)
- walking a dark valley (see *The Dark Night*)
- climbing a mountain (see *The Ascent of Mount Carmel*)
- burning up (see *The Living Flame of Love*)

Although these four images dominate the four different works, they offer parallel descriptions of the same reality, or look at it from four angles. Taken together, they offer the potential for allowing romanticism to be safeguarded by toughness and toughness to be tempered by romance.

Human and divine love

The forty stanzas of *The Spiritual Canticle* are a series of love poems shared between John and Christ. Much of their inspiration lies in the Song of Songs, and John assumes that the relationship between the believer and Christ is like that between two human lovers. That assumption is shared with much of the writings of the mystics.

Is this assumption biblical?

- The Song of Songs does not seem to be about our love relationship with God but about a relationship between two human lovers.
- Where Scripture does talk about our love for God (e.g. Deuteronomy 6:5, John 14:15) it emphasizes commitment rather than emotions.
- Where scripture talks of a marriage relationship with God (e.g. Hosea 1-3), this is between God and Israel or God and the church, not God and the individual.
- Revelation 19-22 sees the consummation of the relationship

Quotations come from *The Collected Works of St John of the Cross*, translated and edited by K Kavanaugh and O Rodriguez, published in 1964 by the Institute of Carmelite Studies, Washington, DC (revised ed., 1991). There are also shorter published selections of John's writings, which will give you their flavour. For instance *St John of the Cross: Songs in the Night*, by Colin Thompson (SPCK, 2002).

The Spiritual Canticle

Growing in a love relationship with God

i Where have you hidden,
Beloved, and left me moaning?
You fled like the stag
after wounding me;
I went out calling you, but you were gone.

vi Ah, who has the power to heal me?
Now wholly surrender yourself!
Do not send me
any more messengers,
they cannot tell me what I must hear.

vii All who are free
tell me a thousand graceful things of you;
all wound me more
and leave me dying
of, ah, I-don't-know-what behind their stammering.

ix Why, since you wounded
this heart, don't you heal it?
And why, since You stole it from me,
do you leave it so,
and fail to carry off what you have stolen?

xiii My Beloved, the mountains,
and lonely wooded valleys,
strange islands,
and resounding rivers,
the whistling of love-stirring breezes,

xiv the tranquil night
at the time of the rising dawn,
silent music,
sounding solitude,
the supper that refreshes, and deepens love.

xx If, then, I am no longer
Seen or found on the common,
You will say that I am lost;
that, stricken by love,
I lost myself, and was found.

xxi With flowers and emeralds
chosen on cool mornings
We shall weave garlands
flowering in your love,
and bound with one hair of mine.

xxiii When you looked at me
Your eyes imprinted your grace in me;
for this you loved me ardently;
And thus my eyes deserved
to adore what they beheld in you.

xxiv Do not despise me;
for if, before, you found me dark,
now truly you can look at me
since you have looked
and left in me grace and beauty.

xxxvi And then we will go on
to the high caverns in the rock
which are so well concealed;
there we shall enter
and taste the fresh juice of the pomegranates.

between Christ and his bride as lying at the end of time, not now.

These passages offer us safeguards against not taking sufficiently seriously before God:

- the importance of commitment in love
- the importance of our corporate relationship with God
- the incompleteness of our experience of God before the End.

There might be two scriptural starting-points for understanding our present individual relationship with God in terms of a love which emphasizes emotion, desire and longing:

- There is one place in Scripture where an individual says to God, 'I love you', in Psalm 18:1. Strikingly, the verb there is not the usual word for love but the word for compassionate feelings such as those of a mother for a child. In Psalm 116:1 the ordinary word for love is used without an object, 'I have come to love because Yahweh listens to my voice.'
- For something more like sexual love with its strength of feeling, see the story of the woman who loves Jesus (Luke 7:36-50). Perhaps it is significant that this is a woman's story; perhaps the absence of this motif from the rest of Scripture reflects the fact that most of Scripture was written by men, given that men often find the expression of affection less instinctive than women do (as in John 21:15-17?).

JOHN'S COMMENTARY

Here is a summary of some of John's comments on his poem:

Seeking to get God to return (on stanzas ii-iv)

- we express our longings and yearnings to try to move God's heart (rather than hiding from them in the pain)
- we ask intercessors to act as go-betweens for us (rather than keeping quiet about our yearning)
- we empty ourselves of other affections and delights, physical, emotional, and spiritual (rather than seeking alternative forms of fulfilment in them)
- we discipline ourselves to a life of love (rather than turn in on ourselves)

In the marriage union with Christ it is possible to 'understand little but love a great deal' (on stanza xxvi). The soul 'easily extracts the sweetness of love from all the things that happen to her, that is, she loves God in them' (on stanza xxvii). 'Even the very exercise of prayer and communion with God, in which she was accustomed to considerations and methods, is now wholly the exercise of love' (on stanza xxviii).

'Let those... who are singularly active, who think they can win the world with their preaching and exterior works, observe here that they would profit the Church and please God much more... were they to spend at least half the time with God in prayer... They would then certainly accomplish more, and with less labour' (on stanza xxix).

'The power and the tenacity of love is great, for love captures and binds God himself' (on stanza xxxii).

THE UNFULFILLED LOVE-LIFE

Like the Song of Songs (and the story in Luke 7:36-50), *The Spiritual Canticle* of John of the Cross presupposes a certain kind of human experience of love. It is not the straightforward romantic process of meeting, getting to know, falling in love, and becoming committed to one another. It is something more complicated or ambiguous.

For some reason these two lovers have to battle to be able to meet. They have to overcome obstacles, and they have to survive frequent partings. They are not married. Consummation is never reached. It may be that the mystical tradition presupposes the monastic experience of deeply-felt but celibate love between monks and nuns.

John's account of the love-relationship of believer and God, and the account in the Song of Songs, presuppose the awareness that the human experience of love may involve features such as these:

- You feel as if someone has inserted a (gentle) dagger into your insides, or you feel as if your beloved has stolen your heart, so that this centre of your being is no longer your own.
- You give irrational priority and effort to meet and spend time with your beloved and you wish you could be with your beloved all the time, but the two of you always have to part.
- You are no longer satisfied with anyone or anything else or with just yourself, but you cannot have a continuous experience of your beloved.
- You wait about where you expect your beloved may be, hoping he or she may appear.

- Your beloved comes your way but doesn't speak to you; you know there must be good reasons, but it hurts.
- Your beloved isn't there when you expect; there will turn out to be an explanation, but you can't imagine what it is.
- Just when you have given up, your beloved is there and your heart is overwhelmed.
- You long to have the words to express the wonder of your love, but you cannot find them.
- When you are together, you grow in understanding of your beloved, but simultaneously you discover that he or she also becomes more and more of a mystery; and the same may be true of your understanding of yourself and of reality beyond the two of you as you look at it through the other's eyes, so that the relationship is one of many-faceted discovery.
- The awareness of the other's unexpected love generates new self-confidence, strength, energy, outgoingness and hope.
- You and your beloved come to influence each other, bringing out likes or potentials which you did not realize were there, and withering other likes.
- From time to time you experience such piercing joy in each other that you feel consumed by the fire; then you have to part again and you have to live with even more intense longing.
- The strength of the feeling of love may be so intense that you wish both to run away from it and to be totally consumed by it.

Each aspect of this experience of human love can have correspondences in our love relationship with God. It may be easy enough to see why some human relationships have to be like that. Why is it is so with relationships with God? Perhaps we simply cannot answer this question; it may be a question like, 'Where does suffering come from?' or 'Why are prayers not answered?' The help Scripture offers lies in resourcing us for living with such experiences and questions, partly by providing us with models for understanding them.

But as with unanswered prayers for healing, one reason for our religious experience being like this is that it is part of the overlapping relationship of this age and the age to come. If the relationship were complete now, this life would cease to be 'not yet'. And one effect of the alternation of presence and absence is that it increases longing for God's presence and joy in that presence; the latter cannot be taken for granted.

JOHN'S COMMENTARY

Here is more summary of John's own comments on his poem:

Stage 1: Love
The most sublime experiences of God's presence never mean that we have finally and incontrovertibly 'captured' God; God remains hidden. Nor need the most arid lack of a sense of God's presence really mean that God is actually absent. The place where God is hidden is in the depths of our own person. We *are* God's dwelling (2 Cor 6:16), whether or not we feel God is there at a particular moment, and whether or not we have sinned.

We will not know the complete fullness or absolute certainty of God's presence till heaven, but we can know it truly if partially and intermittently now. So give yourself to seeking God as the one who lives within. Faith and love are the key.

'Never stop with loving and delighting in your understanding and experience of God, but love and delight in what is neither understandable nor perceptible of him'. When God seems hidden, remember that nevertheless really God is there; when God seems there, remember that God nevertheless remains hidden. Never be satisfied with what you know of God. It is never all there is, so we will always be dissatisfied and longing – whether we feel God is there and want more, or feel God has gone away, and long for a return.

Stage 2: Engagement
With engagement there is still the pain of separation, and there can be strange pressures and temptations to be unfaithful. Yet there is a deeper certainty about the beloved and about the relationship. There is a deep awareness of being loved and of being beautiful, and a delight in offering oneself as beautiful to one's lover. There is a glow about the person which other people can sense. There is a deeper understanding which makes words often less necessary and less useful; a wordless gaze says more.

Stage 3: Marriage
Marriage is not an end but a new beginning. It means

- a once-for-all exclusive commitment and thus a new bravery, a mutual surrender which holds nothing back
- a dramatically new form of oneness such as no words can describe and the finding of shelter and protection from the other
- a mutual attention and esteem, a radical levelling and sharing in which even a 'stronger'/'senior' party makes a 'weaker' party their equal, because that is the nature of love
- an immunity to the disbelief or contempt of others who question the love of the two
- an uninterrupted conversation in which the one has time to reveal everything to the other
- a union of the one with the other in which they come to share each other's natures in intimacy, transformation, and forgetfulness or forsaking of all rival interests and commitments
- a flowering and fruitfulness of oneself in other directions, such as peace, generosity, and bravery.

Stage 4: Consummation
It is a paradox of a developing love relationship such as marriage that for all the closeness of relationship, in a sense the consummation of union is still a goal we long for rather than an experience we reach. The same is true with union with God. Thus with the last stanzas the poem looks forward to union with God in heaven.

There we will be with Christ, will see him face to face, will know as we are known, will know the depths of God's treasures in Christ, will be 'absorbed, transformed, and wholly inebriated in the love of the wisdom of these mysteries' and will hide ourselves in the bosom of the Beloved (on stanza xxxvii). Taught by God's love and responding to it, we will love God as purely and as perfectly as God loves us. 'O souls, created for these grandeurs and called to them! What are you doing? How are you spending your time?' (on stanza xxxix).

GOD'S CREATIVE DARKNESS

It is a common Christian experience that our first years after we come to know Christ (or have some experience of renewal) are full of release and joy. But it is equally common that this is succeeded by a time in which faith and prayer become a battle and our spiritual lives seem to collapse.

St John of the Cross sees this not as a puzzling problem but as an aspect of the way God draws us on. In love for us, God draws us towards maturity, towards closer union.

He distinguishes between two 'dark nights', the first more common than the second.

The Dark Night of the Soul

Our spiritual lives can be characterized by 'spiritual' forms of pride, discontent, lust, anger, greed, envy and laziness. When this is the case, our spirituality is inherently self-centred. God sends the dark night of dryness to draw us on, wanting to relate to us in new ways and to purify us in relation to those spiritual weaknesses.

John's basic advice is that when the spirituality which used to work now fails, we are to do – nothing. The key is quiet, rest, and resistance to the temptation to try to 'do something' in order to reach God. You should think of yourself as an artist's model: what you have to do is sit still for the artist.

This darkness may involve strong temptations of various kinds. At the beginning you may feel little longing or love for God; in due course you may come to feel strong longing. But the old way of feeling is what God is seeking to wean you away from – away from refreshing yourself, so that God can refresh you. The dark night encourages an awareness of your own lowliness and of God's awesome majesty. John sees many passages in the Psalms as illustrating this desert experience (e.g. 51:17, 77:1-6).

Going through this dark night makes a real and permanent difference to your life with God: 'as one liberated from a cramped prison cell, the soul goes about the things of God with much more freedom and satisfaction of spirit and with more abundant interior delight than it did'.

JUST ILL?

John notes that we need to ask, when we seem to be spiritually dry, whether this is really the case, or whether we are suffering from depression or physical illness.

The Living Flame of Love

i O living flame of love
that tenderly wounds my soul
in its deepest centre! Since
now you are not oppressive,
now consummate! If it be your will:
tear through the veil of this sweet encounter!

ii O sweet cautery,
O delightful wound!
O gentle hand! O delicate touch
that tastes of eternal life
and pays every debt!
In killing you changed death to life.

iii O lamps of fire!
in whose splendours
the deep caverns of feeling,
once obscure and blind,
now give forth, so rarely, so exquisitely
both warmth and light to their Beloved.

iv How gently and lovingly
you wake in my heart,
where in secret you dwell alone;
and in your sweet breathing,
filled with good and glory,
how tenderly you swell my heart with love.

The Dark Night of the Spirit

But this may not be the end of the story. Our weaknesses may have been trimmed rather than rooted out and we may become subject to increasing temptations. In due course God may take us into new depths of darkness, dryness, emptiness and anguish.

It is like an experience of death and abandonment by everyone – such as the Psalms describe (e.g. 18:4-6, 88:5-8), Job experienced, and Lamentations speaks of (3:1-20). In due course we will realize that this is a means of receiving great blessing, but at the time that is impossible to imagine. People want to pray, but cannot. And the deepest pain is that they know they love God 'so intensely that nothing else gives them concern… [but] …they are unable to believe that God loves them' because they feel there is nothing worthy of love in them.

The dark night may last years. But in due course it will engender a 'fire and thirst of love' in the deepest part of the soul. Paradoxically, the more God takes away everything, the more chance there can be that God *is* everything. The more we are emptied, the more room there is for God.

This experience makes it easier to press on in the Christian life, because we have dealt with the fear that everything between us and God might be over and lost. 'Love now imparts a force by which the soul loves authentically' with passionate and daring strength. We have been brought to a truly secure resting-place and hiding-place in God.

John speaks of the experience of God's darkness in his poem *The Living Flame of Love*. As happens with the Spiritual Canticle, John appends extensive commentary to his poem.

JOHN'S COMMENTARY

The image of flame suggests that God, out of concern for our transformation, in love acts to burn away parts of us that are incompatible with the likeness of Christ. The process of transformation continues within the context of the marriage-like relationship between us and Christ, on the way to heaven.

It means we think, feel and act like God through sharing in God's life and love. 'The soul… is so inwardly transformed in the fire of love and has received such quality from it that it is not merely united to this fire but produces within it a living flame.' Much of the time the soul remains like 'glowing embers', but when God makes the union actual, the embers not merely glow but shoot forth living flame.

Since the living flame of love 'is a flame of divine life, it wounds the soul with the tenderness of God's life, and it wounds and stirs it so deeply as to make it dissolve in love.' The 'veil' is that which separates this life from the next – so John is asking for death so that he may live the utter life of love of eternal life. His appetite is so whetted by the experience of love now, but is always now frustrated (compare 'now consummate').

'Our God is a consuming fire' (Deut 4:24) – but 'a fire of love, which being of infinite power, can inestimably consume and transform into itself the soul it touches… It does not afflict it; rather, commensurate with the strength of the love, it divinizes and delights it, burning gently.' The burning love of God gains access at one point and is then 'subtly diffused' through the whole being. Thus God 'pays every debt', makes up for all the trials we experience, the disciplines we impose on ourselves, and the darkness we go through. All the effort and pain turns out to be worthwhile.

The 'lamps of fire' (iii) are the different aspects of God's character, such as God's love, power, wisdom and goodness, which illuminate as well as burn, telling you with joy, 'I am yours and for you and delighted to be what I am so as to be yours and give myself to you.'

In order to open ourselves to these we need the 'caverns' of our mind, will and longings to be deep but also emptied – a painful experience which we therefore avoid, preferring to fill ourselves with substitutes. But 'if anyone is seeking God, the Beloved is seeking that person much more.'

MAKING ROOM FOR GOD

There is a further form of darkness. This is the darkness which we actively choose to enter as part of our spiritual growth, as we ourselves take steps to make our relationship with God a closer one.

John offers some principles for making progress in our spiritual lives – principles which show how dark the path to a closer relationship with God is. He urges us always to be inclined:

- not to the easiest but to the most difficult
- not to the most delightful but to the harshest
- not to the most gratifying but to the less pleasant
- not to what means rest for you, but to hard work
- not to the consoling but to the unconsoling...

He further advises us that:

- To come to the pleasure you have not, you must go by a way you enjoy not.
- To come to the knowledge you have not, you must go by a way in which you know not.
- To come to the possession you have not, you must go by a way in which you possess not.
- To come to be what you are not, you must go by a way in which you are not.

There is a strand of Scripture which supports John's negative, self-denying, world-denying stance. It runs contrary to our instincts and culture, but this makes this strand especially worth thinking about – not least when John's suggestions for following it seems outrageous.

Disciplining your desires

John sees renunciation of worldly appetites as the first key stage (the 'evening' at the beginning of the 'night') in making room for God in our lives.

It may help to start from the appetites which emerge in part from our own culture: our appetite for good food, wealth, sex, holidays, parties, sport, companionship, knowledge, affirmation, talking, clothes, books, culture, responsibility, power. We might distinguish several different forms of self-denial with regard to these:

- Sometimes these desires may be inherently wrong – e.g. when they take the form of ambition or lust.
- Sometimes they may go wrong if their influence becomes excessive, as it easily can. In this case, as in the first, we are indeed called to deny ourselves.
- Sometimes we may decide to give up 'normal' appetite for things that are good in themselves (even if they can never 'satisfy'), to make more room for appetite for God.
- John's urges us to be prepared to deny ourselves *all* of them in order radically to make room for God, because even just a small crack lets all the water out of the bucket (see Luke 14:33).

Our various appetites crowd out appetite for God, weary us because of the attention they demand, torment us, obscure our understanding and vision, stain us, and sap our strength. They make us cold towards other people and God. The reason for denying these appetites is not negative but positive – to make room for our relationship with God. Intimacy with God is a supernatural gift, but in another sense it follows naturally from the removal of these obstacles, like the sun shining through a window when it has been cleaned.

Disciplining your mind

Stage two in making room for God ('midnight' rather than 'evening') is the discipline of the intellect or the imagination.

Scripture says that God is light, and that God dwells in darkness. Faith, hope and love therefore involve a journey into darkness – believing what you cannot see, hoping for what you cannot see, loving what you cannot see. 'If the soul in travelling this road leans upon any elements of its own knowledge or experience of God, it will easily go astray or be detained for not having desired to abide in complete blindness, in faith which is its guide.' We do not advance by understanding, experience, feeling or imagination. We have to turn off our own road, from what we find naturally or spiritually intelligible. (See Isaiah 64:4, 1 Corinthians 2:9)

Denial thus involves 'spiritual' matters as much as anything else:

- First, this means not becoming attached to or seeking visionary experiences or messages from God. John talks of 'rejecting' these. This advice may be useful for those of us who view pictures and 'words' positively; there was evidently a lot of charismatic enthusiasm in John's communities. One of his neatest arguments is that such experiences really belong to the old covenant, not the new.

- Second, denial means not becoming stuck in imaginative meditation, because whatever we can imagine cannot adequately represent God. Such meditation is not an end in itself but a means to an end – of being in peaceful repose in the presence of God. So when God draws us into such repose *without* such active meditation, He also calls us to forego it. This advice may be useful for those of us who can get stuck in evangelical or Ignatian Bible study.

John does not write for young Christians. Many people find that God speaks to them powerfully through traditional Bible study and charismatic gifts in the earlier years of their life with God. But many also find that such things no longer work later in their Christian lives, or find themselves drawn into something

less straightforward later. For this, they need to discipline their minds.

John is concerned for such a complete focus on God that all this-worldly awareness disappears – you become unconscious of appetite, sound, touch, time, people, obligations. Initially this may mean you make blunders, but as you mature your closeness of union with God ensures that you are at the right place at the right time, praying for the right people, without your having to sidetrack your spiritual energy by thinking about it.

Disciplining your will

Purifying the will is a matter of giving all our love to God in love's various aspects. Deuteronomy 6:5 is in a sense all you need: 'You shall love the Lord your God will all your heart and with all your soul and with all your might.'

More concretely, disciplining the will is a matter of directing all your passions – joy, hope, sorrow and fear – towards God and not at all towards anything outside God.

John expounds the disadvantages of finding joy in anything

- temporal (status, relationships)
- natural (beauty, intelligence)
- sensory (what we see, hear, touch)
- moral (virtues and achievements)
- supernatural (spiritual gifts)
- spiritual (statues, paintings, quiet rooms, ceremonial, preaching)

All tend to pride and vainglory, and a withdrawal of focus from God.

INCONSISTENT?

John is slightly more positive about the helpfulness of the 'moral' and markedly more positive about the 'spiritual', which can indeed be means of growth. I find this puzzling as it seems inconsistent with the rest of his thinking and I wonder whether he felt unable to disagree with the church's tradition over these means.

SPIRITUAL DIRECTION

There is a personal relationship between each individual Christian and God. Christ has died for each of us and the Holy Spirit lives in each of us. We need no-one to stand between us and God.

Nevertheless we are very likely to profit from talking over our spiritual life with other Christians – peers or someone spiritually older than us. Doctors do not treat themselves or their families, because they are too involved to make sound judgments. Much the same is true in our spiritual lives, no matter how 'far on' we are in the Christian life.

'No one is gifted with such prudence and wisdom as to be adequate for himself in the guidance of his own spiritual life. ... The light of our own judgment is weak and we cannot envision all dangers or snares and errors to which we are prone in the life of the spirit.' John Cardinal Bona, *A Treatise of Spiritual Life* pages 5, 66.

SOUL FRIEND?

Kenneth Leach works with the term 'Soul Friend' rather than 'Spiritual Director'. See his book *Soul Friend: Spiritual Direction in the Modern World* (Morehouse Group, 2001).

What is it?

'Spiritual direction' is a misleading phrase, but no-one has established a better one .

'**Spiritual**' sounds as if it's just concerned with religious questions such as how much we pray, when in fact it is about God's angle on the whole of our lives. It also sounds excessively pious and humourless, when in fact the best spiritual direction is done by those with a sense of humour and a sharp mind.

'**Direction**' sounds as if it means one person telling another what to do or how to live their lives. Think of it instead as a means of 'finding direction'. It's like telling someone where you have been and where you are, and discussing with them the direction in which to go. They are only offering advice – you can always ignore them...

Indeed, often the best thing they do is help us see where we *are*, see the direction our life *has been* taking. This may turn out to be different from where we thought we were (unless we *knew* we were lost...).

Spiritual direction is different from counselling, though over recent decades talking to a counsellor has been as near as many people got to talking to a spiritual director:

- **Christian counselling** starts from particular issues or problems that people have had in their lives, and seeks to help them handle them with God.
- **Spiritual Direction** is concerned with the more general shape of our lives (their direction, in fact). It is designed to encourage us to grow towards maturity in Christ and to move forward on our life's journey with God even if we have no problems. (Ah, if only!) Of course, we *will* have problems, and spiritual direction will work with them, but it is not problem-focused.

Who does it?

Spiritual direction can be done by one person for another, or by several people for each other in a small group. When it's a group, it is often people who know each other already and have built up respect and trust – e.g. the members of a house group. The presupposition is that Jesus is there where two or three people are gathered, and because the Holy Spirit indwells the church, we can be confident that we have the resources to offer interpretation and direction to each other.

You may have access to such a group. If not (and even if you do), you may want to seek out an individual Spiritual Director. You need to think what sort of person might fulfil this role for you. Ideally it needs to be someone who:

- has a living and growing relationship with God
- knows the Bible
- is deeply aware of the fundamental truths of the Christian faith
- has some knowledge of the Christian traditions of spirituality
- understands himself or herself and is discerning about people
- can be trusted to keep confidences
- can trust their own hunches and is bold enough to share them
- you think you can learn from
- doesn't get too much of a kick out of directing people...

It will not be a member of your family or a close friend. It might well be that your own minister fits as much of the above as anyone. Today ministers are being driven from being pastors to being managers, but many would be glad of the opportunity to reverse that process, so give them the chance! There is no great mystique about spiritual direction. It simply needs the capacity to listen to someone and think with them before God about their life.

What happens?

If you are going to see a spiritual director for the first time (or your group is about to meet), it will be an advantage if you have thought through some or all of the following. It may be that the director or the group will want to work in a way which does not immediately take these up, but you will still find them helpful. Write them down, or talk them out into a tape recorder, or tell them to a friend for practice.

- What has been the shape of your life so far? What have been the key events in it, and the key events which specifically involved God? You might tell your story in terms of your Bethlehem, Nazareth, Jordan baptism, Gethsemane, Calvary, Easter, Pentecost (not necessarily in that order).
- What kind of God do you believe in?
- What are the key issues in life for you now? The key joys and sorrows, achievements and failures, challenges and hopes, fears and anxieties? What are your dreams and nightmares (literal and metaphorical)?
- What are the key features of your life as a Christian? When and how do you read the Bible, pray, worship? How do you see your calling and ministry (we all have one!)?
- What are the key features of your lifestyle? How much time do you spend working, and relaxing (and how)?
- What are your key relationships – one-to-one, circles of friends, family, church? What are the enrichments and what are the difficulties in these? How do you think God looks at them?

There is obviously more there than can be written down. You must choose what seems to you to be of key importance. Beware of avoiding things that you know need dealing with – although it is quite reasonable to put some things on hold until you have grown in confidence in your director or your group. (You may also find that they probe areas you have avoided saying something about!)

As you share some of that with your director or your group, they will react, ask questions, pray, seek God, make suggestions... And hopefully you will go away with insights, ideas, hopes and plans.

HOW OFTEN?

There is no 'rule' about how often to meet for Spiritual Direction, but six-monthly is average, especially for individual direction.

A.W. TOZER

(1897-1963)

Aiden William Tozer was the pastor of a church on the same street as some famous blues clubs in Chicago and was also Editor of *The Alliance Witness*, the organ of the Christian and Missionary Alliance. Most of his writings are reprinted from short articles in Christian newspapers and journals. They include *The Divine Conquest*, *The Root of the Righteous*, *Born After Midnight*, *Of God and Men*, and *The Knowledge of the Holy*. What follows is from *The Pursuit of God*.

Believing, then, is directing the heart's attention to Jesus. It is lifting the mind to 'behold the Lamb of God,' and never ceasing that beholding for the rest of our lives. At first this may be difficult, but it becomes easier as we look steadily at His wondrous Person, quietly and without strain. Distractions may hinder, but once the heart is committed to Him, after each brief excursion away from Him the attention will return again and rest upon Him like a wandering bird coming back to its window.

Faith is the least self-regarding of the virtues. It is by its very nature scarcely conscious of its own existence. Like the eye which sees everything in front of it and never sees itself, faith is occupied with the Object upon which it rests and pays no attention to itself at all. While we are looking at God we do not see ourselves – blessed riddance. The man who has struggled to purify himself and has had nothing but repeated failures will experience real relief when he stops tinkering with his soul and looks away to the perfect One. While he looks at Christ the very things he has so long been trying to do will be getting done within him. It will be God working in him to will and to do.

When we lift our inward eyes to gaze upon God we are sure to meet friendly eyes gazing back at us, for it is written that the eyes of the Lord run to and fro throughout all the earth. The sweet language of experience is 'Thou God seest me.' When the eyes of the soul looking out meet the eyes of God looking in, heaven has begun right here on this earth.

When the habit of inwardly gazing Godward becomes fixed within us we shall be ushered onto a new level of spiritual life more in keeping with the promises of God and the mood of the New Testament. The Triune God will be our dwelling place even while our feet walk the low road of simple duty here among men. We will have found life's *summum bonum* indeed.

HANNAH HURNARD

Hannah Hurnard was a CMJ missionary in Palestine earlier this century. She is best-known for her allegory on the theme of the ascent to God, *Hinds' Feet on High Places*, from which the following extract comes. She also wrote a companion allegory on the fruit of the Spirit called *Mountains of Spices*.

The shepherd put His hand in His bosom, drew something forth, and laid it in the palm of His hand. Then He held His hand out towards Much-Afraid. 'Here is the seed of Love,' He said.

She bent forward to look, then gave a startled little cry and drew back. There was indeed a seed lying in the palm of His hand, but it was shaped exactly like a long, sharply-pointed thorn. Much-Afraid had often noticed that the Shepherd's hands were scarred and wounded, but now she saw that the scar in the palm of the hand held out to her was the exact shape and size of the seed of Love lying beside it.

'The seed looks very sharp,' she said shrinkingly. 'Won't it hurt if You put it into my heart.'

He answered gently, 'It is so sharp that it slips in very quickly. But, Much-Afraid, I have already warned you that Love and Pain go together, for a time at least. If you would know Love, you must know pain too.'

Much-Afraid looked at the thorn and shrank from it. Then she looked at the Shepherd's face and repeated His words to herself. 'When the seed of Love in your heart is ready to bloom, you will be loved in return,' and a strange new courage entered into her. She suddenly stepped forward, bared her heart, and said, 'Please plant the seed here in my heart.'

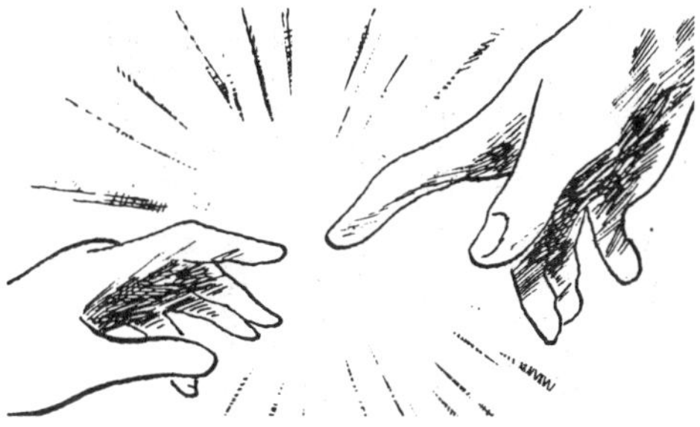

Unit 7

THE WORD MADE FLESH

PURPOSE

This Unit is concerned with the links between our 'spiritual' lives and the ordinary things that make up our day-to-day existence.

It is important for you to relate your spiritual development to the practical realities of human life – such as money, sex and power. Otherwise even a deep and thoughtful spirituality can be accompanied by corruption, immorality and abuse.

CONTENTS

SPIRITUALITY AND FAMILY

If you have had a Christian upbringing, think for a few minutes about what you learned about God from the 'spiritual' side of your family life – things like prayers at bedtime, grace at meals, church involvement as a family. From this experience, what advice would you give to young Christian parents? (If you haven't had a Christian upbringing, what do you imagine is learnt from one?)

✎

Once at St John's we tried to have a discussion of spirituality and the family. I asked several people from staff and student families to share what they had discovered about being a Christian family. It was a sobering experience. Each time I asked, people shuffled their feet, looked embarrassed and muttered that they didn't really think they had found any answers.

I then asked the whole college whether any who had been brought up in Christian families (there were quite a number) could tell us anything that they thought had been helpful to them as they grew up. There was absolute silence.

My wife and I have brought up two sons who are now in their twenties and married. We did the standard Christian things: said grace at meals, prayed and read and sang with them before bed, took them to church and Sunday School and encouraged them to go to youth fellowships. Both have grown into fine young men, one of whom is now involved with church, the other isn't. Reflecting on those years now, I am sure that who we were as parents and the shape of our lives as a whole have affected our sons more significantly than particular things that we did by way of a family prayer life.

In fact, I asked the wrong question of our staff and student families. I should have asked, 'What kind of people were your Christian parents, and how did they relate to you?' And I should have been attempting to look at the question of family spirituality on a broader front.

Family as house church

The expression 'the domestic church' came from Vatican II, but John Chrysostom in the 4th century already described the family as *ecclesia*, church. Families, like churches, can function very differently, but to be faithful to God, each Christian family simply needs to find 'a style of living together under God'.

Husbands and wives need to keep talking about how this works out. Children too need to be part of this conversation – the New Testament declares that the reign of God belongs to the children, and that we have to become like children if we are to draw close to God. Parents learn about God from children as much as children from parents.

Three aspects

The Benedictine tradition of spirituality emphasizes the balance of work, study and prayer. So if family is like church, family spirituality might include:

- **tasks we do together** (chores, care of small children...)
- **learning about God together**: giving children an intelligent understanding of the faith, and learning from them and from our experience of parenthood
- **ways of praying together** (such as thanksgivings and intercessions before the main meal of the day)

Three vows

The monastic tradition as a whole involves three specific vows. We look at these in more detail on the following pages. Each of them can also be reflected in our family life:

- **Poverty**. Money easily becomes a trigger for quarrels and recrimination within the family. Families need to face together questions about shortages and stringency, life-style and priorities. Children may impose pressure on parents to spend what they cannot or should not afford, but families are the context in which they may learn other kinds of delights.
- **Chastity**. Even the Christian family can be the context for violence and abuse, and that needs facing. But the family should be the first context in which we learn to respect other people's integrity, resist the temptation to use others as a means of our self-fulfilment, and delight in giving other people the freedom to be themselves.
- **Obedience**. The old talk of obedience to husbands and parents presupposed a patriarchal structuring of society. A more egalitarian society not only offers partnership between parents, but also reminds us that parents listening to children is as important as children listening to parents. Today children exercise power over parents as well as vice versa, and that power issue also needs addressing with Christian values. The modern Christian family needs to combine structure and power with openness and opportunity for freedom.

Three opportunities

If the family is a small-scale version of a church, then it will have the same opportunities as a church has. Here are some:

- **Ritual and celebration** play an important role for all communities, and not least for families in general and for children in particular.
- The church is **God's servant**, called to serve other people. The family has opportunity to do that as it relates to (say) older people in its neighbourhood who need visits to check out that they are all right, or need shopping or other jobs done.
- **Hospitality** can be an expression of 'family' beyond the immediate boundaries of the family members. While many single people resent it when the nuclear family is treated as a norm by whose standards they are odd, many love being welcomed into the life of a traditional family.

'The family is a place where God's love is made incarnate. Each family is its own ecclesia, a domestic church, with its series of relationships – with each other, with the local community, with God.'

Esther de Waal,
Spirituality in Ordination Training

SPIRITUALITY AND MONEY

Our life with God involves our money.

A book in the Bible which has a lot to say about money is Proverbs. It is a refreshing book to read on money because it recognizes what complex issues money raises.

Proverbs is realistic about how life really works. It does not assume that the invention of the concept of private property is original sin (Karl Marx) or that money is the root of all evil (popular song of the 1950s). It teaches us that money brings security (10:15), popularity (14:20) and enjoyment (21:20).

How to get money

The book of Proverbs encourages us to seek wealth. But how?

- **Be bold** (11:16). Proverbs' advice compares with Jesus' parable about what to do with a bag of gold (Luke 19).
- **Be generous** (11:25). Business involves being sharp, but it also profits from getting on with people.
- **Be honest** (15:6). In a surprising declaration, Proverbs affirms that crime does not really pay, convinced that we live in a moral universe. (Compare 10:2)
- **Be reverent** (10:22). Prosperity comes from God, so continuing to trust God is important (compare 3:9-10). The 'prosperity gospel', like most heresies, gets into trouble by taking one truth out of the context of the rest.
- **Be realistic** (11:24). Prosperity is unpredictable. Even the wisdom of Proverbs is broad generalization, not fixed rules that you can always rely on.

The drawbacks of money

- It has its limitations (11:4). Money can't buy me love or wisdom (3:14) or forgiveness or God.
- It tends to seem all-important (11:28). So don't 'rely' on it – 'rely' on God. You cannot serve two masters.
- It tends to make people forget its moral connections (11:6). The desire for it can makes us overlook our moral obligations.
- It tends to make people forget personal relationships (15:27). If money becomes all-important, it affects friends and family.
- It tends to give people inflated ideas (22:2). We can easily think we are as big as our bank balance.
- It thus tends to drive us to the opposite of the attitudes that will actually lead to making money (generosity, honesty, reverence). So we need to be moderate (30:8-9), with neither too little nor too much money.

How to spend money

The answer to Marx's theory that money causes evil is to do good with it.

- Honour God with it (3:9)
- Serve the community with it (11:26)
- Be generous to the needy with it (28:27, 14:31)

Usually in the world there are people who have no money and people who have lots of it – doing nothing. Proverbs' solution is cash-flow.

Money as God

Martin Luther is supposed have said, 'There are three conversions necessary: the conversion of the heart, mind, and the purse.' In fact it is all one conversion, because money can easily become an alternative god:

- Jesus says we cannot serve God and mammon (Luke 6:13).
- Jesus tells a particular rich man to give everything away if he wants to follow Jesus (Matthew 19:21).
- Zacchaeus' generosity is a sign that salvation has come to his house (Luke 19:8-9).
- 1 Timothy 6:10 says that the love of money is the root of all evil.

Money becomes an alternative god when:

- **we trust in it**. God alone is designed to be the object of the verb 'trust'; but we think that money is security.
- **we gain our status from it**. So the salaries of executives in business have to be far more than they can reasonably spend so that they are shown to be valued.
- **we attach our dreams to it**. In National Lotteries, people hope to win amounts which far exceed what they could ever spend – and which often in fact ruin their happiness.

HOW TO GIVE

Guidance from 2 Corinthians 8-9

For most of us money is an increasing challenge. When we are younger we have relatively little money. We know that nonetheless we had better tithe – and we prove that God looks after us. When children leave and job promotion comes, we have more income and less outgoings. We then have money in the bank – and have to decide what to do with it.

Let giving be an expression of grace (8:1)
Like any other fruit of God's spirit, generosity is an outworking of God's grace in our lives. Giving is not something legalistic. Tithing (giving a tenth of your income) is a good starting-point for giving, but it is not a legal requirement of us.

Let giving be wild (8:2-4)
The Macedonians were profligate, off-the-wall, crazy givers. They were addicted to giving. They begged to be allowed to give, despite the pressure they were under. Giving is not something you start to do when you have enough for yourself.

Let giving be an offshoot of self-giving to God (8:5)
'First they gave themselves to the Lord.' That suggests that he indeed was their God, and Mammon was not.

Let giving be an expression of personal relationship (8:5-6)
They gave themselves 'to us'. At St John's we decide each term where to give away the 'proceeds' of our weekly frugal lunch (usually to two-thirds-world projects). It is projects that people in college are associated with that usually win the vote. We give money to people we can feel in touch with. The Macedonians gave via Paul because he comprised a link with those to whom they gave.

Let maturity in giving parallel maturity in other gifts and fruits (8:7)
A Christian life with a rich set of spiritual gifts is suitably complemented by generous giving. Perhaps there is something odd if it isn't.

Let your giving match the standard set by the generous (8:8)
Paul is not afraid to encourage people to make comparisons and find inspiration from others.

Let your giving reflect Christ's self-giving (8:9)
It seems strange that only now does Paul make this powerful point. As Christ gave up an 'upper-class' position for a low-class or underclass one (Philippians 2), so he gave up riches for poverty. It was the way to lift them from poverty to riches, in accordance with Proverbs' principle of cash-flow. Now they have the chance to be Christ-like.

Let initial emotional commitment become ongoing practical commitment (8:10-12)
It is easy to be moved by some need and then go cold; Paul asks for consistency.

Let giving be the means of producing equality (8:12-15)
Paul would not be satisfied with the situation we experience whereby the haves so outnumber the have-nots. Neither would he let the haves get away with pretending that they don't really have so much.

Let giving be done in the expectancy that God will honour it (9:6-11)
Like Proverbs, Paul believes that giving is good investment. Sacrificial giving is nothing to be afraid of. The people will become 'rich in every way'.

Let giving be enthusiastic rather than reluctant or compelled (9:7)
There are ways of manipulating people to give, and Paul could be thought to be using them in these two chapters. But in the end he wants individuals to come to their own decisions about what to give.

Let giving be such as will glorify God (9:12-15)
Paul's hope is that the Corinthians' giving will amaze other people and be recognized as a fruit of the Spirit, so that it will bring God glory.

SPIRITUALITY AND SEX

Thinking about sex in connection with spirituality is different from thinking about sex in connection with ethics. Here we are not primarily concerned with the rights and wrongs of different forms of sexual activity. We are thinking of why and how sex matters to us as people, and how sex thus impinges on our relationship with God.

Much that follows applies to the marriage relationship in particular, but our sexuality is broader than our involvement in sexual acts. So much of what is said here also applies to other relationships between men and women, and between people of the same sex.

Sex and God

When Genesis 1:27 says that we were created in God's image, it immediately adds that we were created male and female. An implication of this is that it is male and female together who image God. The way we relate to each other as men and women is designed to reflect something of God's nature and to be reflected in the way we look after the world on God's behalf. So our sexuality is really important to our living for God and with God.

To begin with, the different-ness of man and woman has the capacity to begin to image something of the different-ness within God. The writer of Genesis did not know about the Trinity, of course, but the Trinity makes the point about that different-ness within God. Men and women are called to rejoice in their different-ness and make the most of it – rather than try to avoid it because it can be uncomfortable. In doing so, they discover something of who God is, and together they image God in the church and in the world.

Sexual relationships give us a particular and powerful opportunity to image God's character to one another. Sexual relationships involve issues of power and control, and the temptation is to exercise them in ways other than God's. According to Ephesians 5, the way a husband exercises power (acts as head) is not by giving orders but by giving up himself for his wife, loving her as he loves himself. The way a wife submits to her husband is by letting him do that.

In sexual relationships we also image God's faithfulness and compassion. As God never gives up on us, like a mother in relation to her children, so we never give up on those with whom we have a sexual relationship. Of course such statements about God are balanced by other statements that indicate that God can reach a point where enough is enough. This happened with northern Israel, whom God abandoned to defeat and exile – recorded alongside the motherly testimony of God in Hosea 11. Women and men too may sometimes have to say 'Enough is enough' – and can do so in ways that reflect God's faithfulness and compassion.

The importance of sex

People say that sex matters in our culture more than it has in others. It may be that we are simply less restrained in talking about it. Either way, sex is important because you cannot be a human being except in relationship with other people – and sexual relationships are among the most powerful of relationships. Such relationships affect us very deeply, and in any culture these relationships will matter.

There is of course a purely physical element to the longing for a sexual relationship. But when people have physical sex, they do so as whole people, bodies and hearts and minds. Bodily coupling is an expression of the coupling of the whole person, and the longing for it is a part of the

THE POTENTIAL OF SEX

The joke says that after sex, men want to sleep and women want to talk. But after sharing sex, even men are more likely to share deep feelings, doubts and questions. Sex can be an expression of power and violence, but it can also be an expression of vulnerability, both for men and for women – and it may make other forms of vulnerability possible. In doing so, it makes growth possible too. Accepting physical touch often opens us up to being touched emotionally.

SELFISH 2-SOME?

Being in love can make people turn away from other relationships into an *egoïsme à deux* (two people in a self-centred two-some). Or it can make them turn outwards towards other human beings and God with new energy. If it is the latter, a sexual relationship can issue in human creativity which also glorifies God, consciously or unconsciously.

hunger for intimate relationship. We long for the sense that another person knows and loves us and that we know and love this other person.

There are other reasons why sex is so important in modern society. With the breakdown in many forms of relationship in our culture (e.g. in extended families and local communities), we are all looking for relationship and love. That puts extra pressure on marriage relationships – so much hangs on them.

And in a culture where God has little significance for people, a heavier weight falls on sexual relationships, on the person who is the sole 'significant other' for them.

Sex and worship

Our sexual relationships have the capacity to be profound whole-person relationships. They are very obviously body-matters, but the people involved in the physical coupling are mind and heart as well as flesh, and mind and heart can be involved in their coupling.

Your relationship with God is also a profound whole-person relationship. It is obviously a mind-and-heart matter, but as a human being you are involved in this relationship as flesh as well as mind and heart, and you relate to God as flesh. So speaking, hand-waving, singing, foot-tapping, shouting, smiling, kneeling, crying and laughing are all involved in worship (well, they would be if our worship were more biblical), as they are in love-making (well, some of them...).

We can speak of our relationship with God in sexual terms; and we can speak of our sexual relationships in worship terms. It may be that as individuals we are better at one than at the other. Perhaps we are invited to learn how to do the one *from* the way we do the other – to let the depth and the freedom we have in the one become true of the other.

Life without sex

Celibacy often releases energy into other relationships of love, both with other people and with God. We have seen that reflected in our study of St John of the Cross. People who are celibate (that is, committed to living without a physical sexual relationship) may have quite intense but chaste relationships with each other and may be quite intense in their relationship with God. (There is not the slightest implication that they lack the sexual potential of someone who is sexually active – just as being married doesn't mean you have no sexual hang-ups or problems.) Perhaps that is one significance of the way in which the Song of Songs, those poems about an elusive human love, have been so treasured as expressing the nature of our love for God.

So our sexuality can reflect and resource our relationship with God, even when we do not have a physical sexual relationship within which to express it.

Sexual healing

Sex is an area where many of us (maybe all of us) need healing. In this it is just like every other area of life; the difference may be that we have not been able to talk about it. Men need this healing in their way, women in their way.

Our prayers about sex, too, can be redeemed. They are not merely prayers of confession regarding the guilt of our feelings, longings and actions. They can be prayers of delight, joy and thankfulness. And they can be prayers of anxiety, sadness and longing. (See James Nelson, *The Intimate Connection*, SPCK, pages 116-117).

THE PAIN OF SEX

For all sorts of reasons, talk of sex may be painful for you. You may only cope with God by dissociating God from sex. As a coping mechanism, that's fine. Bear in mind that one day you may be in a position to look more into the abyss of that hurt, and that that may be creative as well as painful. Today may even be the moment to begin. (But it may not. Ask God.)

'Sex is a parable.'

Jim Cotter, *Pleasure, Pain and Passion: Some Perspectives on Sexuality and Spirituality* (Cairns Publications, 1993)

SPIRITUALITY AND FOOD

FOOD FOR THOUGHT

For a more detailed discussion of the place of food in Christian theology, see *The Task of Old Testament Theology* by Rolf Knierim (Eerdmans) pages 225-243.

There is no doubt that food relates to our life with God.

In the Lord's Prayer we ask three things for ourselves:

- food for the day
- the forgiveness of our sins
- protection from temptation

– in that order. Christian theology has discussed the doctrine of forgiveness endlessly, and Christians pray fervently to be protected from temptation. But we are weak in our understanding of food. Perhaps this is why thousands die each day of hunger, while the largely Christian nations have more food than they can eat. Had we taken this clause of the Lord's Prayer more seriously, we might have developed a doctrine of food supply for all humanity.

Enjoying food

The Bible begins with God creating food (admittedly vegetarian food, it seems). Page after page of the Old Testament rejoices in festive eating, in meals and in hospitality. The requirements of Exodus, Leviticus and Deuteronomy closely associate food with Israel's life as God's people:

- Almost any worthwhile worship occasion involves a meal with God (because this is what is involved in sacrifice).
- Never an animal is killed for food without offering it to God.
- Never a harvest is enjoyed without offering the first fruits to God.

The way in which some foods were allowed and others forbidden was designed to make food part of what made Israel Israel, and witnessed to its distinctive relationship with God and its calling.

In the religious culture in which the New Testament was written, there were people who required abstention from marriage and from some foods, as an expression of rejection of this-worldly things. In contrast, 1 Timothy 4:3-5, 6:17 states key principles which are implicit in Genesis:

- food is something 'which God created to be received with thanksgiving...
- 'everything God created is good, and nothing is to be rejected if it is received with thanksgiving, because it is consecrated by the word of God and prayer.'
- 'God... richly provides us with everything for our enjoyment.'

Abstaining from food

Periodic abstention from food is a common practice in Old and New Testaments as in other religions. The significance of fasting for us as Christians needs to be seen in the context of the enthusiasm for food which characterizes biblical faith.

I had never understood fasting. I had thought that the point of fasting was to enable greater concentration on God in prayer. I couldn't imagine that this would ever work for me – I would be thinking about my empty stomach rather than concentrating on prayer. And I was troubled that there seemed to be nothing in the Bible that suggested that this was the point of fasting, even if some people did find that it helped them pray. Then I realized that the significance of fasting lay elsewhere.

A good way into understanding prayer is to think about the various ways in which human beings communicate with each other; we can then apply those to our communication with God in prayer. Similarly, a good way to understand fasting is to think about why in ordinary life we sometimes don't eat.

In ordinary life we abstain from food for a number of reasons:

- **Grief**: for example, it is common for bereavement to take away appetite.
- **Concern** (in particular, worry) about something can put us off our food.
- To **focus** on work, people may go without lunch.
- We may abstain from some foods to keep our weight down or to **train** for maximum performance in a sporting activity.

Fasting makes these kinds of abstention part of our relationship with God. So in the Bible people fast for a similar range of reasons:

- **Grief**: fasting was a natural accompaniment to repentance for sin; see Jonah 3, Zechariah 7-8. It went with other signs of grief such as the wearing of mourning clothes. *Fasting shows that we really are grieved.*

- **Concern**: fasting could accompany the search for guidance and the prayer for equipping (Acts 13:1-3, 14:23). It accompanies prayer for oneself (2 Samuel 12:15-23, Ezra 8:21-23) and for other people (Psalm 35:13, Ezra 10:6). *Fasting shows we really are preoccupied.*

- **Focus**: fasting made possible Jesus' forty days in the wilderness (Matthew 4) and Daniel's seeking of God (Daniel 10). *Fasting shows that something else really is important.*

- **Training**: fasting is frequently spoken of as self-denial (so Leviticus 16:29-31, 23:26-32), getting on top of our bodily desires. *Fasting shows that we really do control our body, rather than the other way round.*

There may well be benefits to body and mind through fasting. Some people also believe it helps prayer. But prayer is not necessarily the accompaniment of fasting; the two are essentially separate activities. Fasting is an outward expression of grief or concern, or a way of focusing or training, whatever it does to my concentration on prayer.

There are no rules about how long we should fast, or precisely what counts as fasting. Scripture provides examples of going without one meal and of fasting for forty days. Partial abstention is another pattern, like having just a sandwich for lunch (see Daniel 10:2,3). The Muslim pattern of fasting during the day but eating after sunset, recalls 1 Kings 17:6. Normally fasting does not mean abstaining from liquids (but see Ezra 10:6).

SELFISH FAST?

Isaiah 58 is a suggestive passage which denies the validity of fasting when it is accompanied by self-indulgence and exploitation in other areas. Fasting is a form of self-denial and a symbol of self-denial – so the person who fasts properly, will be sharing freedom and food with others.

SPIRITUALITY AND POLITICS

'[God] teaches us the language of the kingdom by providing us with the psalms, which turn out to be as concerned with rough-and-tumble politics as they are with quiet waters of piety.'

E. H. Peterson, *Where Your Treasure Is: Psalms that Summon You from Self to Community*

Politicans tend to run the world on one of the following assumptions:

- God does not exist ('The fool has said in his heart...').
- God has set the world going but left its running to us.
- God is involved in the world and is on our nation's (even our party's) side. In Britain, the church was defined as the Tory Party at prayer – more recently, as the Labour Party at prayer.

Our discussion of spirituality and politics starts from four rather different convictions:

- the world is God's and God cares about it.
- politics is important but it is not everything.
- the world is not what it claims to be.
- worship is a key activity in creating a new world.

Psalms and political change

The book of Psalms denies that the world is as it claims to be. With extraordinary boldness, Psalm 95 declares that Israel's God, Yahweh, is the great God and is the great King.

For most of their life it looked as if the great **god** was Baal, Marduk or Zeus – the god worshipped by people who were their cultural, political or military superiors. But Israel declares that in the real world Yahweh is the great God.

For most of their life it looked as if the great **king** was someone such as Sennacherib, an Assyrian king who claimed exactly that title. In their worship the Israelites denied his claim. They asserted that the real world was not the one you read about in the papers, but the one you heard about and sang about in worship.

Convinced that in the real world Yahweh was God and King, they could go out into the apparent world about which they read in the papers and behave in it as if it were indeed the real world – with the possibility of its then becoming the real world.

Paul's way of making this same point is to urge us not to be conformed to this world but to be transformed by the renewing of our mind (Romans 12:2).

Bringing in the Kingdom?

Christians often talk of working for the advance of God's kingdom, for the coming of God's rule. I don't think the Bible talks in this way. In Scripture it is God who brings in God's reign. Scripture doesn't think that we do anything about that.

Except pray.

I believe that Christians should work for justice in society. The prophets, the lawgivers and the sages of the Bible did that. But they did not refer to such work as bringing in God's kingdom. The fact that they didn't use such language, and that we do, are both significant.

The day after the election of a Labour government in Britain in May 1997, after 18 years of Tory rule, there was considerable euphoria. I expressed unease at the idea that a change of government was going to bring in the kingdom. A woman at a lunch at our church said, 'I have just begun to hope and you are taking my hope away.' I was unrepentant. Hope based on a change of government is no hope.

Power to change

Christian people are trapped by guilt and by powerlessness as they contemplate the situation of the world. This is so whether we look at inequality within our own society, at the oppression of the two-thirds world by the first world, at the arms trade, the threat of terrorism, the two-thirds-world debt, or the poor wages paid to tea-pickers in Sri Lanka.

To express our awareness of guilt, and to work against our powerlessness, we sign petitions to parliament and we boycott particular companies. We must do something. But the actions and their effectiveness cannot match the extent of the guilt and the powerlessness. Even people involved in business and politics feel that they themselves share in the powerlessness. The problem is bigger than them.

In the martial arts, people use their opponent's destructive power to their own advantage. So we may be able to use the spiritual force of guilt and of powerlessness to bring our prayer alive.

- **Guilt**: we need to face guilt more seriously, rather than being content with a generalized, perhaps neurotic, guilt awareness. Let's look at the *actual and personal* greed or stereotyping or aggressiveness or defensiveness which the problems noted above can draw attention to. We can then begin to repent of those and seek new life in Christ in respect of them.

- **Powerlessness**: we have to ask whether we actually believe that God has power and that prayer might be the means God has given us of releasing God's power into the world.

'You lead me by still waters.'

Praying for your nation

In his book *Where Your Treasure Is: Psalms that Summon You from Self to Community* (Eerdmans 1993), E. H. Peterson urges us to pray the Psalms as a political action. 'Prayer was [the Psalmist's] characteristic society-shaping and soul-nurturing act.' He encourages us to study 'eleven psalms that shaped the politics of Israel and can shape the politics of America':

2	the unselfing of America
87	unself-made
110	unself-centred
93	unself-government
46	unself-help
62	unself-assertion
77	unself-pity
14	unself-righteous
82	unself-serving
114	unself-sufficient
45	unself-love

He then suggests a way of going about it. He suggests corporate prayer, because the Psalms are designed for corporate, not individual, use.

- Gather a few friends and commit yourselves to meet together for the 'unselfing of America' (or of Britain or wherever)

- When you meet, pray the Psalm. Discuss its application to your nation; pray it again. Spend time in silence letting it soak in; and pray it a third time.

- Look for God to draw you into action.

For the idea of using guilt and powerlessness to pray for and to being about political change, see Charles Elliott *Praying the Kingdom* (DLT, 1985) page 2.

SPIRITUALITY AND DISABILITY

A longer version of what appears on this subject here appears in a book on theology and disability, *Encounter With Mystery*, ed. F M Young (DLT, 1997). For more detail on some topics, see J Macquarrie, *In Search of Humanity* (XPRESS Reprints, 1993), especially pages 47-58; and W Pannenberg, *Anthropology in The Biblical Perspective* (Continuum, 1999), especially page 82.

There are 'normal', ordinary ways of being human, and there are non-standard ways. The lives of people with physical and/or mental handicaps may be in some ways very different from the 'ordinary', but such people are just as much genuinely human beings.

In meeting a disabled person I meet someone else made in God's image. Their differentness contributes to my understanding of what it means to be human, and what it means to be God.

The diversity within humanity reflects our being made in God's image, it reflects the diversity within God, Father, Son and Holy Spirit. When abled and disabled live, work, and worship together, humanity is represented in a greater fullness and God is imaged.

My wife Ann is disabled. Most things I have learned over recent years about God and about how we relate to God, I have learned through being married to her.

A different dominion

Human beings have a task to perform. We are designed to have dominion in the world. The abled can learn from the disabled how to go about creativity, world-making, control, authority, as well as vice versa. We are all made in God's image.

In particular, the disabled reveal to humanity a facet of being human from which the abled can often hide – weakness, vulnerability and dependence. The disabled are characterized by vulnerability and have the capacity to call forth enormous love; in doing so, they embody aspects of the nature of God which humanity is called to image in its controlling of the earth. They embody the fact that there is sometimes a mysterious power in poverty, vulnerability and weakness, a power to move and transform.

The presence of disabled people amongst us also draws our attention to the fact that the exercise of control, the activity of creation, occupies six days but not seven. The climax of creation's story lies in a rest from activity, such as the disabled may be constrained to accept. The disabled invite us to the play, spontaneity and impulsiveness which are also part of being human.

Being Christian depends upon trust – we are justified by faith. But being human at all depends on trust. We cannot be self-sufficient in relation to other human beings, let alone to God. The disabled embody that fact about being human.

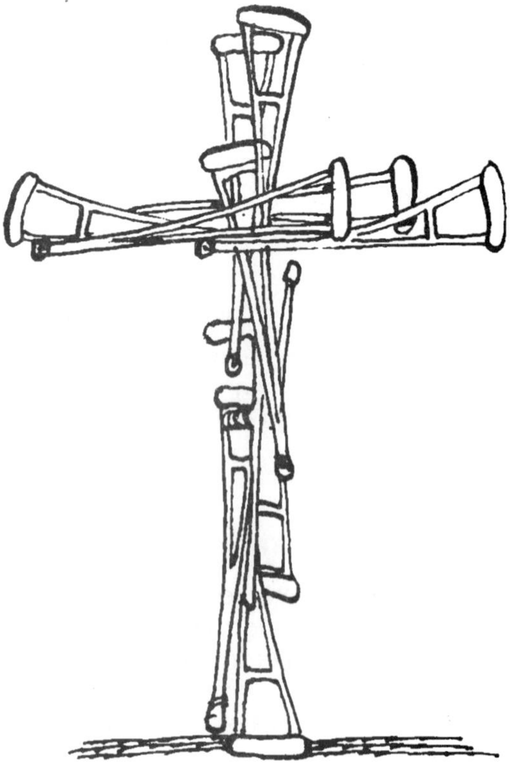

A clearer journey

Because the abled are the norm, we may think we define real normality and we may thus assume that we represent full humanity and creativity. Disabled people minister to us by making more obvious a truth which applies to us all – that we have not arrived. Full humanity lies ahead of us, in the resurrection of the body which transforms the whole person so as to make us fully human. The little experiences we have now, the little steps that we take, are steps *towards* full humanity, as the Holy Spirit has God's way with us and brings about some anticipation of resurrection fullness.

When a disabled person who has been neglected or institutionalized is befriended and known, that person can change and grow. When a person becomes disabled, that takes them onto another journey which can look (and probably is) more painful but which can also involve breathtaking transformation. The former may be led from bondage to freedom. The latter may look as if they are on the way from freedom to bondage, but may be able to own their changing humanity in such a way as to make it a new (and sometimes deeper) form of freedom.

The lives of disabled people illustrate how part of the mystery of human individuality is that it is not static and unchanging. Their lives are manifestly journeys – ours are just less clearly so.

A need of 'other'

Disabled people draw our attention to the fact that human beings are designed to live in relationship. They may sometimes illustrate that negatively, by their unhappiness and frustration at not being in relationship. They certainly do it positively, by their uninhibited joy in relationships, by their lack of self-sufficiency which makes them more evidently in need of relationship in order to live at all, and by their capacity to draw others into relationship.

On a gloomy day I reflect that (in some North Atlantic cultures, at least), it seems women want to be in relationship only with other women, and men do not want to be in relationship… It can seem easier for women to relate to other women, for men to relate to other men, for like to relate to like, for abled to relate to abled and avoid disabled – and in some ways for disabled to relate to disabled. At the day centre for disabled people to which my wife once belonged, I was struck by the sense of community and relationship based in part on what people had in common. But the presence of disabled people amongst us remind us of the point that Genesis 1 hints at, that some of the most fruitful relationships involve difference.

A wholeness of body

The disabled draw our attention to our ambivalent relationship to our bodies. Our bodies are not just the shell within which the true person is found, but neither are they the precise embodiment of the person. There is something miraculous about the way in which in each person freedom, transcendence and rationality are conjoined with a material organism. Disabled people help us to avoid the tendency to exaggerate spirituality and rationality so that we forget the material. They teach us to laugh and to cry – and to surrender to our bodies, to surrender control of our 'selves' to them.

Disabled people also remind us that being human, being in God's image, is a corporate affair. The points which Paul makes about the church as the body of Christ apply also to the body of humanity. There is no unity in identity, only in diversity. The disabled contribute their gifts to this body, and none is to be despised – even if we have no right to insist that they themselves view their disability as a gift to them. We and they must recall that whatever parts we are inclined to view as weak and foolish therefore possess particular glory and dignity (see 1 Corinthians 12:22-24). Thus communities which exclude disabled people are disabled communities.

(1745-1832)

HANNAH MORE

Hannah More was a voluminous writer, but better-known for her social activism as an 18th/19th century evangelical. The excerpts which follow come from J. M. Gordon's *Evangelical Spirituality*.

On 6 April 1807, the Eclectic Society, a group of Evangelical clergymen meeting in London, addressed the question, 'How may pious women best subserve the interests of religion?' Simeon notes, 'The generality seemed to think they did best by keeping at home and minding their own business. My ideas did not perfectly coincide with theirs'. One woman who neither kept at home nor minded her own business was Hannah More.

...Later, having suffered the humiliation of being jilted three times, she was compensated with an annuity for £200 and used her financial independence to make lengthy visits to London.

...Her plays, directed and produced by Garrick in the Drury Lane Theatre, made her a much sought-after London celebrity. More thrived on witty conversation and the intellectual give and take of late eighteenth-century London, but after some years disenchantment began to surface in her letters.

The world applauded much of More's literary work; Christian friends repeatedly praised her for the great good done by her writings, often falling into the same sin of uncritical flattery which she found so objectionable in the world; she played hostess to a constant stream of bishops, literary figures, Christian workers, friends and strangers, on one occasion noting ruefully that she had nineteen visitors, six of whom she had never met before. More was too honest not to recognize the dangers of such admiration; and too scrupulous to enjoy it innocently.

...Conflict with 'the world' presented a further spiritual dilemma; how to serve God in the world without being contaminated by its values. Does obedience to God involve separation from, or involvement in, the world? Attracted to a life of retreat, quiet study and spiritual cultivation, she was impelled by an equally powerful need to work towards her optimum level of usefulness for God. Inevitably she was torn between the conflicting, and often contradictory, demands of being and doing.

William Wilberforce had a galvanizing effect on Hannah More. Through him she became deeply committed to the abolition of the slave trade. On principle she boycotted West Indian sugar and carried a plan of a slave ship with which she ruined many an evening planned by unsuspecting hostesses for agreeably harmless conversation. Between 1788 and 1805 she published several works in which she criticized the morals and manners of 'the Great'. The *Estimate of the Religion of the Fashionable World* and *Strictures on the Modern System of Female Education* caused offence to some, but became very popular with the upper classes. Westminster schoolboys burnt an effigy of the woman who had dared write about 'the dissipation of youth'.

During the 1970s More and her sisters, at the instigation of Wilberforce, had begun a programme of basic education amongst the mining families and villagers of Cheddar. The scheme spread to cover many villages all over the Mendip Hills, so that by 1796 over 1600 were enrolled in ten parishes.

AND YOU?

Particular areas or issues in life can for each of us be the catalyst for significant spiritual growth. Look back over the six issues dealt with in this Unit. Is there one of these which might be a creative point of spiritual growth for you at this point in your life? Or can you think of another issue that would? Choose something that *matters* to you.

✎

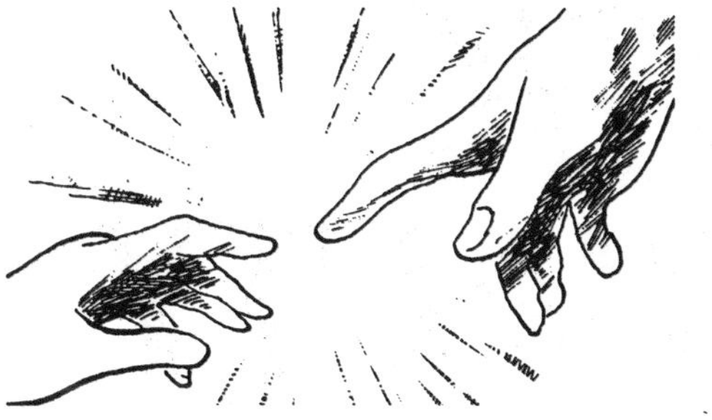

Unit 8

LESSONS FROM THE PRESENT

PURPOSE

This Unit looks at some of the ways people, in the past and today, have formed a spirituality that relates to the big issues of life.

As you reach the end of the course, it is important that you do the same. What can you learn from these spiritualities? And what are the 'big issues' against which you are going to develop your life with God in the coming years?

CONTENTS

CELTIC SPIRITUALITY

When the gospel reached Britain, it found a lively natural religion in the Celtic fringes of Britain – in Ireland, Scotland and Wales. In these country regions, God's presence was seen in every spring, river and lake. In everyday life, God was seen as involved in blessing all the key events of life – birth, marriage, moving house, dying.

This religion was converted to Christ rather than destroyed. As a result Celtic Christianity is distinctive for its affirming of God's involvement with creation. God is involved at each moment of a day. There are prayers for getting up, getting dressed, lighting the fire, setting off for work, milking, grinding, weaving, fishing, sowing, harvesting, coming home, eating, and going to bed. God is the transcendent Lord, but one immanent in the world.

Celtic Christianity was in no danger of a dualistic separation of God and the world, of sacred and secular, of body and soul, of heart and mind. God was 'in all things'. Celtic spirituality thus invites people to see God in creation and to see creation as God's.

ANCIENT AND MODERN

The story of Celtic Christianity centres first on St Patrick, who gave up his home in Scotland to spread the gospel in Ireland in the 5th century. In the 6th century St Columba made this journey in the other direction and settled on Iona. In the 7th century Aidan then took the gospel back from Iona to northern England and established his monastery and missionary centre at Lindisfarne. It was Celtic Christianity which thus flourished as the rest of Europe was entering 'the Dark Ages'.

The person who is indispensable to the modern revival of Celtic spirituality is Alexander Carmichael, who lived and worked as a tax man in the Scottish Isles in the 19th century. All over, but especially in the Outer Hebrides, he collected the hymns and prayers of the people's everyday life.

Celtic and Christian

When Christianity embraced the traditions of the ancient Celtic religion, it did not lose sight of the gospel of Christ.

- Celtic Christianity was enthusiastic in its love of the Scriptures, as is illustrated by decorated gospels such as the Book of Kells.
- It has instinctively lived in relationship with God as Trinity, as is illustrated by the classic Celtic hymn *St Patrick's Breastplate*.
- The same hymn emphasizes the reality of forces of evil which could threaten us, but also emphasizes the effectiveness of the protection available to us.
- Celtic spirituality is not romantic about nature. For the people who practised this faith, life was generally demanding and often cruel. Perhaps this is why in recent years it has rung bells with people immersed in the poverty of the inner city.

Celtic spirituality represents a distinctive weaving of various strands of Christian tradition:

- In its earliest centuries Celtic spirituality was influenced by the Eastern desert fathers; Egyptian monks visited Ireland.
- Its affirming of 'natural religion' and its historical links with Pelagius give it affinities with liberal Christianity.
- Its enthusiasm for holy places, pilgrimage, and for bodily expression in worship (in genuflexion, stretching out the arms to form the shape of the cross, raising eyes and hands to God), gives it affinities with catholic and charismatic spirituality.

Blessing of the kindling

I will kindle my fire this morning
In the presence of the holy angels of heaven.
In the presence of Ariel of the loveliest form,
In the presence of Uriel of the myriad charms,

Without malice, without jealousy, without envy,
Without fear, without terror of anyone under the sun,
But the holy Son of God to shield me.
   Without malice, without jealousy, without envy,
   Without fear, without terror of anyone under the sun,
   But the holy Son of God to shield me.

God, kindle Thou in my heart within
A flame of God to my neighbour,
To my foe, to my friend, to my kindred all,
To the brave, to the knave, to the thrall,
O son of the loveliest Mary
From the lowliest thing that liveth,
To the name that is highest of all.

Blessing of a house

Be Christ's cross on your new dwelling,
   Be Christ's cross on your new hearth,
Be Christ's cross on your new abode,
   Upon your new fire blazing.

Be Christ's cross on your topmost grain,
   Be Christ's cross on your fruitful wives,
Be Christ's cross on your virile sons,
   Upon your conceptive daughters.

Be Christ's cross on your serving-maid,
   Be Christ's cross on your knee of promise,
Be Christ's cross on your coming generation,
   Upon your prospering cattle.

Be Christ's cross on your means and portion,
   Be Christ's cross on your kin and people,
Be Christ's cross on you each light and darkness,
   Each day and each night of your lives,
   Each day and each night of your lives.

Celtic Threes

Three sisters of lying: perhaps, maybe, guess.

Three sisters of youth: desire, beauty, generosity.

Three sisters of age: contentment, chastity, gentleness.

Three things that bring relief: a servant laying down his load; a traveller taking off his shoes; a good man approaching death.

Three sources of new life: a woman's belly; a hen's egg; a wrong forgiven.

Three people whose ears are closed: a king bent on conquest; a merchant bent on profit; a monk who thinks himself holy.

Celtic wisdom

There is a mother's heart in the heart of God.

To go to Rome*
   Is much trouble, little profit.
The king whom thou seekest there,
   Unless thou bring Him with thee,
   thou wilt not find.

* It would be wise to add Jerusalem and Galilee, Iona and Lindisfarne, of course.

Night Prayers

O God of life, darken not to me Thy light,
O God of life, close not to me Thy joy,
O God of life, shut not to me Thy door,
   O God of life, refuse not to me Thy mercy,
   O God of life, quench Thou to me Thy wrath,
   And O God of life, crown Thou to me Thy gladness,
O God of life, crown Thou to me Thy gladness.

I lie down this night with God,
   And God will lie down with me;
I lie down this night with Christ,
   And Christ will lie down with me;
I lie down this night with Spirit,
   And the Spirit will lie down with me;
God and Christ and the Spirit
   Be lying down with me.

MORE?

These and many other Celtic prayers can be found in:

A. M. Allchin and Esther de Waal, *Threshold of Light* (DLT, 2004)
Esther de Waal, *The Celtic Vision* (DLT, 1989)
Robert Van der Weyer, *Celtic Fire* (DLT, 1990)

LIBERATION SPIRITUALITY

The theology of liberation was born in Latin America in the 1960s. It took as its starting point certain revolutionary convictions:

- God is committed to the poor
- the church should be too
- we should expect God to act to deliver the oppressed
- the church should commit itself to that deliverance.

In *A Spirituality of Liberation*, Pedro Casaldáliga and José María Vigil suggested the following marks (among others) of the spirituality that will express and undergird such commitments and understandings.

Spirituality must start from reality

Sometimes spirituality can be an escape from real life. Religion can be a drug to keep the poor in their place. An inner life with God can be a way of hiding from what is going on in life.

Liberation theology insists on facing facts and looking for their causes so that we can get to the root of problems. It insists that in our life with God we face the fact that other people are treated unfairly. Far from withdrawing to find God, it expects to find God by deliberately seeking to share the experience of the poor, with whom God identifies.

Liberation spirituality then reacts with 'ethical indignation' to what it sees. It does not accept things or remain unmoved. Alongside indignation is compassion, a feeling of the world's pain as our own.

Liberation spirituality lives in festival and dance, joy and song

Our diocese has a link with the Diocese of Teso in Uganda. One expression of that involved a mixed-race teenager from our congregation joining in a group visit from our diocese to theirs to help build a school. Ian was bowled over – not just by the toughness of rural life in Uganda, but also by the joy which characterized their life. Although materially they had so little, their lives were much happier than ours.

Likewise the people of Latin America live in festival, dance and song. Their lives are shot through with festivity. Neither hunger nor struggle nor natural disasters prevent them from organizing a dance at the first opportunity; all their mourning and all their striving is done to singing. They move from tears to laughter as the most natural thing in the world.

Spirituality, hospitality and generosity

In Britain we have to lock our doors and bar our windows, and we are more and more separating into one-person households. The community has disappeared. In Uganda, Ian was struck by people's hospitality. They had hardly anything, certainly not enough for their needs, but they instinctively shared it. They live without calculation.

Where contemplation takes place

In a spirituality of liberation, contemplation takes place not by withdrawal or by an inner journey, but in the midst of the process of liberation, with its convulsions and risks. The object of our contemplation is indeed the things of God, but the things of God are the things God is doing *in this world*.

The reign of God is God's sovereignty being implemented in the world. We can love this world because God is active in it, fulfilling a purpose. We do not assume that everything is achieved in this world, but we look for the fulfilment of God's purpose not merely in heaven but also in this creation which belongs to God.

Our prayer is for that reign of God to come on the earth, as Jesus taught us to pray. This prayer is to 'Our Father': we pray it with all God's sons and daughters. So prayer incorporates the horizontal with the vertical.

Contemplation can be an attitude of *tranquillity* in God's presence, without images, focusing on God's purpose or reign, on God's works in life, from the core of the person. It can also be a sort of *disturbance* which harmonizes with God's own compassion, with God's holy wrath. It shares the sufferings of human beings and of God. It takes on ourselves the experiences our brothers and sisters are going through.

All this is not to imply that everything is prayer. Action is action and prayer is prayer. But these two belong inextricably together; they are the inside and the outside of the same reality.

The option for the poor

The option for the poor is a distinctive mark of liberation theology and liberation spirituality. It means that we encounter Christ in the poor, recognizing features of his suffering in theirs. We actually find Jesus in them. In this sense they evangelize us.

- We find our discipleship in relation to them, acting in relation to them in the manner of the Jesus we follow.
- We discover a principle of Christian discernment here, a principle which plays a key role in our discerning where the truth of God really lies. In particular, it enables us to see where lie the limitations in some of the traditions of spirituality.
- We rediscover the meaning of charity, which includes individual kindness but goes beyond that to a desire for the creating of just structures in society.

All this involves not a rejection of the members of the dominant classes but a rejection of their attitudes and mind set. It involves an exodus and an incarnation. It involves actively taking up the cause of the poor – and accepting the destiny of persecution and martyrdom which goes with that.

Sin and conversion

We began with realism. This realism includes a recognition of our personal sin in resisting God's reign, a recognition of the way in which sin affects the structures of society, and a recognition of the way in which these two interact.

Conversion needs to correspond to sin. It involves being 'turned' upside down and inside out. It involves
- an everyday turning to God
- an everyday turning in welcome to others, especially the poor
- an everyday turning to ourselves, to strengthen the roots that feed our essential commitment
- an everyday turning to Jesus' cause.

CREATION SPIRITUALITY

There are pitfalls in every movement in spirituality. The nature of heresy is to take a half-truth and treat it as the whole truth.

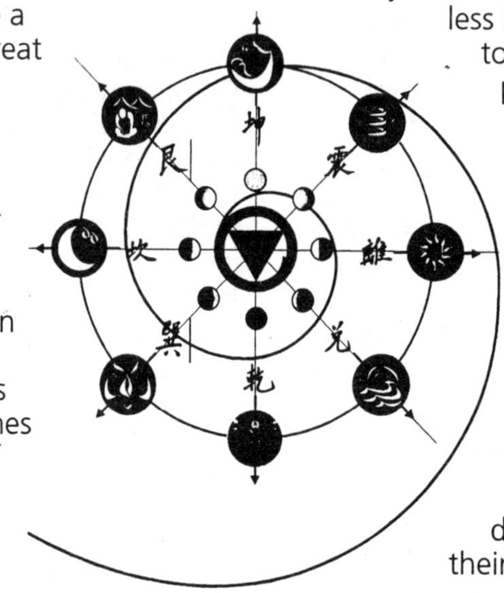

If creation spirituality is taken as the answer to everything and in isolation from much else in this course, it becomes a heresy. But if we set creation spirituality in the context of the gospel of Christ's death and resurrection (as Celtic spirituality did), there is much we can learn from it.

A key writer in this area is Matthew Fox, whose books (*Creation Spirituality*, *Original Blessing,* and others) have been very influential.

Suburban liberation?

We have noted that the lives of people in Africa and Latin America often combine material impoverishment with inner joy. In the Western world many people have their bodily needs (food, housing, health care) well met, but they are deeply unhappy. The problem of the one is an impoverishment of the body, of the other an impoverishment of the spirit.

Deprived urban areas in the Western world may be more like the two-thirds world (in both the good and the bad ways); liberation spirituality may have something important to say to them. That spirituality is less likely to speak directly to affluent suburban people – except simply to challenge them to identify with the poor.

Fox suggests that creation spirituality is a liberation spirituality for the suburbs. Here the rich and the comfortable (for whom Christ also died) may find help for their souls.

Creation and spirit

Creation spirituality emphasizes our oneness with creation as a whole. It is this which makes the despoiling of creation wrong – it is like sinning against our own family.

While the Bible clearly distinguishes humanity from the rest of creation (only human beings are made in God's image), it identifies humanity and creation more clearly than we often do.

- The animals as well as humanity are indwelt with God's breath and created by means of God's spirit (Psalm 104:30).
- The creation of humanity is the climax of the creation story in Genesis 1, but three-quarters of the chapter is occupied with the rest of the cosmos: planets, plants, fish, birds and animals.
- The last day of creation is to be a day of rest for the animal creation as well as for humanity (Deuteronomy 5:14).

CREATION THEN AND NOW

- In the Bible, creation is sometimes something God did thousands of years ago, in first bringing the world into being.
- Sometimes creation is something God is doing *now*, in restoring Israel or renewing the church. It is something God is continuously doing, simply in keeping the world in being.
- Creation is also something God *will* do, in bringing into being a new heaven and earth.

Psalm 104 provides a good illustration of the way the Old Testament speaks of God's creative activity in relation to the world – at the beginning and every day, without really distinguishing them.

It is also striking that in the creation narrative the word 'spirit' is linked with the process of creation. This suggests that our 'life in the Spirit', our spirituality, should be too.

The spirit of creation is life, breath, and wind. To be spiritual is to be full of life, breathing deeply, carried by the wind.

Creation spirituality also sees our creativity, our activity as human beings, as a continuing of God's creativity – indeed a *sharing* in it as people made in the Creator's image.

The four paths

Creation spirituality presupposes that we can learn about life from sources outside Christian faith – that God did not leave the peoples of the world without some knowledge of God. This can be a misleading assumption if we make too much of it, but it is a view which fits with the Bible. The 'Wisdom Books' (such as Proverbs) assume that it is possible to learn things about how God works, from the world as we experience it. The books about worship (such as Leviticus and the Psalms) reveal that Old Testament worship was not wholly different from the worship of other peoples.

What we learn from the world and from other peoples needs to be set in the context of our distinctive Israelite and Christian faith. But as long as we do that, there are things to learn.

Partly on the basis of such resources, Fox suggests that creation spirituality involves a journey along four paths. Each path:

- tells us one thing that matters
- tells us one place where God will be found
- gives us a commandment.

❶ The path of affirmation

The first path affirms that awe and delight matter. Wonder at the mystery of nature and of all beings is appropriate because each is 'a word of God', 'a mirror of God that glistens and glitters' (Hildegard of Bingen). The commandment is to fall in love, at least three times a day, with some part of creation.

❷ The path of denial

Path two declares that darkness, suffering and emptying matter. God can thus be found in nothingness, pain, silence, letting go, and letting be. The commandment is to dare the dark, to enter the covered-up parts of ourselves and of our society – its evil, and our apathy, anger, despair.

AN EXODUS STORY FOR OVER-DEVELOPED PEOPLES

Fox suggests that creation spirituality has a potential to liberate 'first world' people, parallel to the potential of liberation theology for two-thirds world people. Both offer an experience of liberation reminiscent of the Old Testament Exodus.

Creation spirituality offers us liberation:

• from the secularization of everything	to the resacralization of all things
• from boredom and passivity	to wonder, creativity, and empowerment
• from taking for granted	to thankfulness
• from waste	to recycling
• from tiredness	to youthfulness
• from complacency	to compassion
• from art for art's sake	to art for earth's sake
• from fundamentalist fear	to trust of the cosmos
• from 'I think therefore I am'	to 'creation begets therefore we are'
• from theism	to mystical panentheism (everything is in God)
• from institutionalized religion	to living mysticism
• from sexism	to gender justice
• from unemployment	to good work
• from humanity-centred, hierarchical capitalism	to earth-centred economics
• from the fantasy dream-life of advertising	to an authentic vision of a just new creation.

❸ The path of creativity

Path three declares that creativity and imagination matter. In our generativity we co-create with God. 'We are heirs of the fearful creative power of God' (Eckhart). The commandment is that we should not be reluctant to give birth. Such creativity is not so much about painting a picture as about naming our shadow side.

❹ The path of transformation

The fourth path affirms that justice matters. We find God in working to relieve suffering, to combat injustice, and to bring about balance in society and history, We find God too in the celebration which happens in the midst of that. The commandment is to be compassionate as our Creator in heaven is compassionate.

MORE?

For more on a theology of God which is sensitive to environmental concerns,see *Sustaining the Earth* by Tim Cooper (St John's Extension Studies) chapter 3.

FEMINIST SPIRITUALITY

I am grateful to Gillian Cooper for this account of feminist spirituality, and to Ollie Harrison for his account of male spirituality.

What is feminist spirituality? The word feminist implies taking women's experience seriously – in this case, women's experience of God. It involves asking whether it is different from men's.

Women may relate to God differently from the way men do, because:

- they have experienced the world differently
- they have experienced their upbringing differently
- God has usually been conceived of as male (and therefore unlike them)
- Jesus was male (and in this sense unlike them).

Feminist spirituality is concerned to claim a tradition. It knows that there is a tradition of women's spirituality within the Bible and in Christian history, and it wants to explore it.

RELIGIOUS OR CHRISTIAN?

One result of the focus on women's experience is the tendency for feminist spirituality to cross boundaries between faiths. At an earlier stage, Christian feminists were inclined to celebrate Jesus as a liberatory figure over against his Jewish background, but they have now retreated from that kind of discussion. Identity as a woman may seem more important than a particular faith-allegiance, and there are overlaps of interest with wicca, new age spirituality and goddess-figures. So as well as making for common cause between women in different Christian denominations, feminist spirituality encourages common cause between Christians, Jews and Muslims.

Feminist spirituality uses women's experience to reflect on God and on our relationship with God.

The question I have to handle is whether I can meet God as a woman in the context of the church. The patriarchal nature of the church makes me tempted to think I cannot, but I cannot get away from the conviction that the gospel is true and therefore I can only stick with it.

Mothers

Margaret Hebblethwaite (in her book *Motherhood and God*) looks at God in the light of the experience of motherhood. But is motherhood the defining characteristic of women? This is not always so for women who *are* mothers, let alone those who are not. Feminist spirituality is not centrally about calling God 'Mother'.

Whereas I find talk of the motherhood of God unhelpful, I find women's prayers helpful. There are examples in Janet Morley's *All Desires Known*.

The body

The stress on women's experience also encourages a spirituality which affirms the body. It is a non-dualistic spirituality. Women are particularly aware of the physical, of their bodies and their bodily cycles. They are more inclined to see the self as an integrated whole. In worship they are more likely to enjoy the sensate and the symbolic (for instance, the use of candles).

Equality

Feminist spirituality has a sense of justice and maintains a commitment to justice. It believes in a God of equality and justice. So it has a view of God and of humanity's relationship to God which sees women as equal partners with men.

The use of inclusive language (avoiding the use of the word 'men' as if it meant all human beings) follows from that. Language helps us think about God in ways that see women sharing fully in humanity with men.

Play

In her book *A Big Enough God*, Sarah Maitland has a playful attitude to theology and spirituality. She is able to be playful partly because it has been men who have been the guardians of the spiritual traditions, so women are freer to play with ideas and to access the playful side to God. Stories are then the way into such theology and spirituality, as in Maitland's *Angel and Me*.

A shared experience

Christian faith is a matter of the corporate, not merely of me and my relationship with God. It is about relating to God with others, and not least with other women. One result is that I find that I am not alone on my journey with God.

MALE SPIRITUALITY?

Is there such a thing as male spirituality?
The idea might seem almost self-contradictory:

❶ Throughout western history men have been the dominant sex. This has blinded men to any critical appraisal of themselves in terms of their gender.

❷ The mystical and spiritual has often been cast in feminine terms. We think of the church, the people of God, in a female frame of reference, as Christ's adoring and dependent bride. From the ancient Israelites onward, Western spirituality has thought of humanity's relationship with God as analogous to that of a woman's relationship with a man. The mystic is sensitive, passive, receptive, unpredictable – in short, a woman.

❸ In recent times feminist theology has been influential in shaping spirituality. There has been little attempt by men to respond to this thoughtfully and thoroughly. Some men simply accept the feminist critique unconditionally, others retrench against it. This is now changing, and asking what is distinctive about male spirituality is part of that.

❹ Men have been challenged by a broader and more secular feminism within the academic disciplines. The emergence of women's studies as a distinct and defined field has prompted men to see themselves as men. They have begun – however informally and tentatively – to invent men's studies. The study of male spirituality exists within (or between) men's studies and theology.

Men such as James Nelson are beginning to write about male theology and spirituality – e.g. *The Intimate Connection* (SPCK) and (with Susan Longfellow) *Sexuality and the Sacred* (Mowbray). But traditionally texts about spirituality by men (including the Bible) have inevitably not thought of the question. They come from a pre-men's-studies sense of maleness, and assume that being a man in the male sense is simply being a man in the human sense. It is thus anachronistic to read them too much in the light of our own time. But we may be able to see them as subconsciously providing patterns of masculinity, even though only now do we look at them in that light.

Male spirituality has to come to terms with the male identification with power and oppression. This gave a special flavour to the sense in which men had fallen out of 'right-relationship' – first with God, then with others, and finally with their own selves. It has to come to terms with the identification of *eros* and needfulness. And it has to cease splitting off matter from spirit.

Male spirituality needs to be doing three things:

- engage feminism in a constructive critical dialogue
- propose new ways of being male
- be expressed in men's relationships with other men, with women, with God, and with creation.

ANGLICAN SPIRITUALITY

LEARNING FROM DIFFERENCE

Each Christian denomination is a resource for the spirituality of its members, but also provides another model of spirituality which those in other denominations can learn from. In this workbook I am not seeking to cover the spirituality of each denomination, but here is an attempt to think about mine (with some help from an address on the subject by Gordon Mursell – see box).

- You might like to see whether there are resources for you here, especially if you are not an Anglican.
- What would be the equivalent things that you could say about your own denomination?

Corporate
Anglican spirituality emphasizes the church itself. (If we have prayed with the church, why do we also need to pray on our own?)

Liturgical
Anglican spirituality is structured and liturgical. It assumes that there is a shape to prayer, and that prayers composed by other people can be true expressions of *our* prayer. They help us to express what we need to say.

Traditional
With the rest of the 16th century reformation the Church of England rejected the medieval church, but it still valued Christian tradition. In developing new forms of service, they made creative use of the way Christians over the centuries had prayed.

Comprehensive
The Church of England has often been called the 'middle way'. In practice it can be a haven of safety and moderation, with enthusiasm always held back by reason. But its commitment to comprehensiveness can hold diverse positions together (like the four we considered in Unit 1) so that all are enriched.

Aesthetic
The Church of England inherited great medieval cathedrals and developed their worship. It provided a home for poets and writers from John Donne to C. S. Lewis. It became a patron for the work of composers such as Charles Villiers Stanford, Herbert Howells and Herbert Sumsion.

Musical
From the beginning the Church of England's worship included the sung as well as the said. Plainsong, Anglican chant, hymnody, anthems and the organ are among the forces which in the past have contributed to making the Church of England's spirituality what it is.

Priestly
It is said that the Reformation did not go far enough, because it retained the 'priestcraft' of the medieval church under a new name. The Church of England walks the tightrope of retaining an ordained priesthood without compromising the priesthood of Christ and the priesthood of the whole church.

Eucharistic
The Book of Common Prayer suggested a Sunday worship pattern of Holy Communion, Morning Prayer and Evening Prayer. This plan of Cranmer's was always unrealistic. Last century Holy Communion started to take a more central place in Anglican spirituality, Christ offering himself not merely in words but things we see, touch and taste.

Calendrical
Anglican spirituality affirms the Church's Year, reliving each year the story of creation, the preparation for Christ's coming, incarnation, ministry, crucifixion, death, resurrection and giving of the Spirit. It is also a lectionary church, systematically submitting itself to scripture as a whole.

Located
The Church of England centres on buildings. Its great cathedrals suggest the awesome transcendence of God by their magnificent architecture. Its parish churches locate the church at the centre of each community.

Praying the 'Offices'

Daily Anglican worship is characterised by the 'offices' of Morning Prayer and Evening Prayer. This was a simplification of the *seven* offices which shaped the day in medieval monasteries, in order to provide a pattern of prayer for ordinary people.

It became part of Cranmer's *Book of Common Prayer* ('common', to serve all the people) of 1662. Their structure and essential nature survived into the offices in the *Alternative Service Book* (1980) and *Common Worship* (2000).

Anglican clergy are supposed to say Morning and Evening Prayer every day (in practice most say Morning Prayer most days). Some will say the offices in church, as Cranmer intended, so that lay people can join them. Cranmer required that the church bell be rung so that people could also join in at a distance.

Some clergy say Morning Prayer on their own as the framework for their Bible reading and prayer. But they do so knowing they are part of a large communion of saints who are praying the same prayers and reading the same passages.

If you commit yourself to this form of prayer

- ask God to speak to you through the worship – and then listen
- don't worry if this doesn't happen every day – you have still worshipped
- give yourself time to get into this form of worship – most people need time.

'Office' ingredients

- The opening verses and responses put God on our lips right at the beginning, open ourselves to God's help if we are to worship at all, and give us chance to encourage each other to worship.
- The Psalms are scripture's own manual of prayer and praise, so that we train ourselves in the prayers that need to be prayed. We are not choosing what to say but discovering what God invites us to say.
- In the reading of scripture we work systematically through the whole Bible, so that it has opportunity to shape our thinking and our lives. Worship is an opening of ourselves to have our faith formed by scripture, rather than by what *we* think God is saying now, or by our favourite passages.
- A 'canticle' links us to the early days of the church's worship, joining in the worship of the whole church going back two millennia. Such material from *outside* the Bible reminds us that the church has the freedom to form its own words to God in response to what God does for us.
- The creed can be said as an act of praise rather than merely a statement of theoretical beliefs. And it is another reminder of the alternative way of looking at the world that our faith commits us to, in contrast with the worldview within which we will live the rest of the day.
- The prayers begin with the Lord's Prayer, given by Jesus as a model. The 'collect' puts into words to God the calendar theme for the week. And the closing collects make bridges into the life we live outside worship. We can incorporate into these prayers others for the world's needs, the church's and our own, and also our response to what the Scriptures have had to say.

COLLISION

by Gordon Mursell

We accept the Church's lectionary and the portion which we are to read. That has remained a constant in the Anglican spiritual tradition. Similarly the Psalter has been something which was 'given'. You read chunks of it. You did not just pick the bits you liked. You did not go into church and say, 'Well, I feel angry tonight, so let's pray Psalm 109.' You went in and you would pray what was given to you. This used to drive me scatty when I was a young curate in Liverpool, when you could not just pick the bit you liked. You were stuck with it. Now I am immensely grateful for it, because it seems to me that at the heart of liturgical Anglican spirituality is collision... In the best Anglican spiritual tradition your feelings will collide with what is given to you in the Word, and whether you like it or not, you somehow have to make something creative out of the collision between your excitement and enthusiasm and the sort of intense introversion of Psalm 119, or the collision between your furious irritability with your rector or whatever it is and the ebullience of Psalm 16. There is something about that collision which seems to me Anglicanism at its very best.

MORE?

For more detail on worldwide Anglicanism and its spirituality, see *Something in Common* by Adrian Chatfield (St John's Extension Studies).

AMY CARMICHAEL

(1867-1951)

Amy Beatrice Carmichael went to India as a missionary in 1895 and founded the Dohnavur Fellowship, which provided a home and Christian upbringing for children in the Tirunelveli district of South India. Many of her published works are poems and letters, many of the latter written during years of illness. Like Francis Ridley Havergal (see page 24), she felt that her poems and songs were not so much written, as 'something for which we put out our hands, as it were, and take.' These excerpts are from *Toward Jerusalem* and *Edges of His Ways*.

TOO GREAT FOR THEE

An angel touched me and he said to me,
The journey, pilgrim, is too great for thee,
But rise and eat and drink,
The food is here,
Thy Bread of life,
Thy cruse of Water clear,
Drawn from the brook, that doth as yesterday
Flow by the way.

And thou shalt go in strength of that pure food
Made thine by virtue of the sacred Rood,
Unto the Mount of God,
Where thy Lord's face
Shall shine on thee,
On thee in thy low place,
Down at His feet, who was thy Strength and Stay
Through all the way.

O Cake of Bread baken on coals of fire,
Sharp fires of pain,
O Water turned to Wine,
The word is true, this food is daily mine;
Then never can the journey be
Too great for me.

IF IT WERE NOT SO

I thought I heard my Saviour say to me,
My love will never weary, child, of thee.
Then in me, whispering doubtfully and low,
How can that be?
He answered me,
But if it were not so
I would have told thee.

I thought I heard my Saviour say to me,
My strength encamps on weakness – and so on thee.
And when a wind of fear did through me blow,
How can that be?
He answered me,
But if it were not so
I would have told thee.

O most fine Gold
That nought in me can dim,
Eternal Love
That hath her home in Him
Whom seeing not I love,
I worship Thee.

Here is something I read lately and enjoyed:

A centipede was happy till
One day a toad in fun
Said, 'Pray, which leg goes after which?'
Which strained his mind to such a pitch
He lay distracted in a ditch,
Considering how to run.

I think there are a good many toads in the world, and sometimes, not in fun at all but very seriously, they manage 'to strain our minds to such a pitch', that instead of going on in simplicity we may very easily find ourselves distracted in a ditch, not running, but only considering how to run.

But this need never be. In one of the loveliest nursery pictures, we have our God teaching His little child how to walk, taking it by its arms as one does in teaching babies: 'When Israel was a child, then I loved him, ... I taught Ephraim also to go, taking them by their arms;' it is all there – 'With human cords used I to draw them, with the bands of love'. So did we learn to walk in our Father's nursery; and now that we are out of the nursery and on the race-course – *looking away* (the only time that word occurs in the New Testament) from toads without and within – let us *run... looking unto Jesus*, our Faith's Princely-Leader-Perfecter. So shall we run and not be weary, and walk and not faint.

REGISTERING FOR SUPPORT

If you would like the help and support of a tutor in developing your life with God, please fill in the form below. We will link you with one of our tutorial staff. You may photocopy this form if you prefer.

I want to study **The Vital Connection** with tutorial support.

Name
Address   Postcode   Telephone

I enclose a cheque for £50.00 to cover the cost of distance tuition.

Please use the space below to tell us about yourself: something about your background and why you are interested in doing this course. It will be useful to your tutor to have this information.

Send this form, with your remittance, to: St John's Extension Studies, Bramcote, Nottingham NG9 3RL. Telephone 0115 925 1117 for enquiries and credit card payments. You can fax this form on 0115 943 6438.

OTHER WORKBOOKS IN THE FAITH FOR LIFE SERIES

GOD THOUGHTS

Engaging with the modern world using the skills of theological reflection

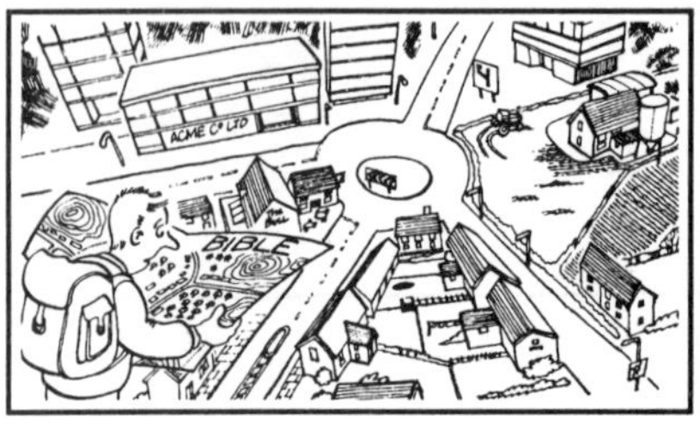

Ian Aveyard

A workbook for those who want to learn how to think more clearly as Christians – not just theoretically, but in ways that will help them make better Christian decisions. These decisions may be about their personal lives or about the big issues that confront our culture. All such decisions are affected by how we see God – our images of God and our assumptions about how God acts in the world. If our assumptions are mistaken, we are misguided in our Christian thinking and we make poor decisions.

Some people call this 'theological reflection', a phrase sometimes used in this workbook. Don't be intimidated by such terms. 'Theology' is something which every Christian does, whether they realise it or not! We all have our 'God Thoughts'.

The only question is how *well* do it. This workbook is for those who are ready to do some hard work in order to do their theology – and live their Christian lives – better.

Sometimes this is hard *intellectual* work, because woolly thinking leads to poorly-focused theology and bad Christian decisions. But it is also hard *personal* work, being honest with ourselves and with others about how we really think and feel about God and the Christian life.

We say that some people have a 'calling'. God showed them that He wanted them to be a missionary, a minister, a monk. The calling was clear, the step that needed making was clear, and they took it. Now they have a vocation.

For many of us that is not our experience. It's not that we love God less, or are unwilling to make sacrifices. We have some sense that God is calling us – to something. But it is not at all clear.

The issue of Christian calling are not always well taught. The remarkable 'calls' of the great saints are held up as the ideal. And calling has been seen in highly individual terms, dwarfing the calling of the Church as a whole.

God has purposes in this world and calls each of us to become part of them. We need to understand those purposes, and see where we fit within them.

This workbook enables you to
- understand the kind of life God calls His people to live.
- think about the place of the Church in working out God's kingdom purposes.
- discover where you and your gifts fit in – including whether you might indeed become a missionary, a minister or a monk or nun.

It will help you become fit for that purpose. Often we need to grow to be the 'shape' God needs for a particular role. You will also be helped by the optional weekend conference.

FIT FOR THE PURPOSE

The meaning of Christian vocation and how to respond when God calls

Ian Aveyard and David Muir

Also available

Leading Children
Understanding the children of today, and bringing the Christian faith to a new generation

In Search of Wholeness
A Christian theology of healing, and practical training for church and medical settings

The World Christian
For those who want to learn to live as members of the worldwide church

Entering Another's World
For those who want to know how to live for God in another culture

Sustaining the Earth
A Christian approach to caring for the environment

Something in Common
An introduction to the principles and practices of worldwide Anglicanism

The Distance Learner
A travel guide for Christians studying theology

PRICE: £10.95 (POST FREE) PHONE 0115 925 1117 FOR CREDIT CARD SALE